Kitchen Glassware

of the Depression Years

Fourth Edition

By Gene Florence

COLLECTOR BOOKS

P.O. Box 3009
Paducah, KY 42001

The current values in this book should be used only as a guide. They are not intended to set prices, which vary from one section of the country to another. Auction prices as well as dealer prices vary greatly and are affected by condition as well as demand. Neither the Author nor the Publisher assumes responsibility for any losses that might be incurred as a result of consulting this guide.

About The Author

Gene Florence, born in Lexington in 1944, graduated from the University of Kentucky where he held a double major in mathematics and English. He taught nine years in Kentucky at the junior high and high school levels before his glass collecting "hobby" became his full time job.

Mr. Florence has been interested in "collecting" since childhood, beginning with baseball cards and progressing through comic books, coins, bottles and finally, glassware. He first became interested in Depression glassware after purchasing an entire set of Sharon dinnerware at a garage sale for $5.00.

He has written several books on glassware: *The Collector's Encyclopedia of Depression Glass*, now in its ninth edition; *Elegant Glassware of the Depression Era*, now in its third edition; *The Collector's Encyclopedia of Akro Agate;* *The Collector's Encyclopedia of Occupied Japan*, Volume I, II and III; *Very Rare Glassware of the Depression Years* and the *Pocket Guide to Depression Glass*, now in its sixth edition. He recently completed the second edition of his innovative *Standard Baseball Card Price Guide* which has been very well received in card collecting circles.

A very special milestone for Mr. Florence occurred in 1988. Collector Books announced that his books have sold over a million copies since the first *Collector's Encyclopedia of Depression Glass* was published. Should you be in Lexington, he is often found at Grannie Bear Antique Shop located at 120 Clay Avenue. The shop (site of his mother's former day-care business) derived its name from the term of endearment toddlers gave her.

If you know of any unlisted or unusual pieces of kitchen glassware of the type shown in this book, you may write him at Box 22186, Lexington, KY 40522. If you expect a reply, you must enclose a self-addressed, stamped envelope – and be patient. His travels and research often cause the hundreds of letters he receives weekly to backlog. He does appreciate your interest, however, and spends many hours answering your letters when time and circumstances permit.

Acknowledgements

The culmination of three years of effort to improve this book was vastly aided by many collectors and dealers who need special thanks – from those who shared collections to be photographed or aided in pricing, to those who helped in the actual photographing or publishing. We all endeavored to make this book the best in its field. The pictures alone are the result of a four-day photography session in California, several days in Ohio and five or six sessions in Paducah. My son Chad attended his first (and probably last) photography session in California. His assistance (from driving hundreds of miles to arranging photographs) was greatly appreciated.

A very special thanks to Terry and Celia McDuffee who opened their home and lives for the photography invasion. (The transformation of a workshop into a photography studio is quite an undertaking.) Unpacking all the glass reamers and measuring cups the day of a major earthquake was also quite an experience for them! Too, they spent hours on the phone helping to price and to obtain information to get this mountainous task finished.

Thanks to the following for lending glass, help in photographing or pricing information: Bill Schroeder, Dave and Barbara Hammell, Kenn and Margaret Whitmyer, Dan Tucker and Lorrie Kitchen, Nancy Maben, Hank and Carla Bowman, Don and Sally Davis, Judy Smith, Stanley and Louise Duda, Bob and Carole Radcliffe, Edna Barnes, Arland and Marjorie Stokes, Melvin and Linda Sumter, Michelle Rosewitz, Steve Quertermous, Tom Clauser and numerous other collectors who have written me or shared information at shows for the benefit of fellow collectors.

Words can't express my gratitude to Della Maze of Collector Books for her help in deciphering the "mazes" of a new computer program for this book.

Thanks to the family, Cathy, Chad and Marc; Gene and Gladys Florence (Grannie Bear) and Charles and Sibyl Gaines who have weathered the ordeals of travel and deadlines!

3

Foreword

The comment I have heard again and again at shows concerns the availability of kitchenware. There are numerous pieces seen over and over, but the already hard-to-find items are showing up even less frequently. This happens in all fields of collecting. The choice pieces are bought up by serious collectors and until that collection is sold or broken up, many rarely-found items are not on the market at any price. It takes patience as well as money to collect. One of the joys of collecting is finding that special piece that you have been seeking for a long time. It can make your day!

In the three years since I wrote the third *Kitchen Glassware of the Depression Years*, I have been asked time and again, "When is the next book coming out?" Writing a new book is a lot like collecting. Choice items for new pictures may be few and far between. It was difficult to find enough different items to justify a new book until recently. So please enjoy these 4,500 pieces of kitchenware! It's more than ever shown before, and getting them here was by no means an easy task! I hope you'll find all the effort taken was worth it!

I have observed that more collectors are gathering kitchenware by colors than any other way. Because of this, **colors** are the first listing in this book with **items** and **patterns** following. I'm aware this causes some overlapping of photos and information, but it was done in order to please collectors and couldn't be helped.

Pricing

All prices in this book are retail prices for **mint condition** glassware. This book is intended to be only a **guide** to the prices. A price range has been given for kitchenware items to allow for some wear and a little roughness that is normally not allowed in collecting other forms of Depression Glass. You will note that the price range has been widened in several areas, but particularly in reamer and measuring cup collecting. I have received pricing ideas from over a dozen dealers and collectors and the range of pricing was enough to blow my mind. Since I, ultimately, must take the brunt of pricing discrepancies from collectors and dealers alike, I want you to know that the only rule in pricing seems to be determined by who owns it and who wishes to own it. In other words, only **two** people determine price, the buyer and the seller. You, ultimately, have to decide if the price is right for you.

The roughness or usage marks found on Kitchenware is a turn off to some collectors who search for perfection. Remember, these were utilitarian items and were in use for years; therefore, most collectors will allow some roughness. This does not mean cracks, chips and chunks are acceptable. To the contrary, these greatly reduce the value of a piece. It simply means that kitchenware collectors are a little more lenient about the condition of the glassware than are collectors of Depression dinnerware. They have to be because most of the kitchenware does not exist in absolutely mint condition!

I have seen both higher and lower prices for most items shown; however, the prices listed are prices that collectors somewhere in the country have been willing to pay.

Colors

Any time the word green or pink occurs, it means a transparent (see-through) color. Other color items are described below.

Amethyst – a transparent, violet color.

Black Amethyst – color appears black but will show purple under a strong light.

Blue – "Chalaine," an opaque, sky blue made by McKee; "Cobalt," a transparent, dark blue; "Delphite," an opaque, medium blue made by Jeannette.

Clambroth – translucent off white or translucent green.

Custard – an opaque beige.

Green – "Jad-ite," an opaque green made by Hocking; "Jadite," an opaque green made by Jeannette; "Skokie," an opaque green made by McKee.

White – milk white; milk glass; opal white (All these terms simply indicate a white color); "Vitrock," a white made by Hocking.

Yellow– vaseline, a transparent greenish-yellow; "Seville" yellow, an opaque yellow made by McKee.

Contents

Part 1 – Colors
AMBER (Dark)

This book is divided into three sections: **Color**, **Items**, and **Patterns**, in that order. Some items are pictured more than once, and hopefully, the prices are the same in each case of a repeated item. I spent hours trying to make certain of that. However, feel free to report any discrepancies you find.

There are hundreds of new items shown in this book; but in order to make room for them, some entries previously shown had to be omitted. I assumed that you would prefer to see new items rather than a different display of those seen before. However, for those persons discovering Depression era Kitchenware for the first time, we've still included all the basics again.

Amber is not the most avidly sought color, but many pieces are rare. Reamer, measuring cup and knife collectors are having difficulty finding those pieces in amber for their collections. Many Fry collectors would love to have the reamer or the tray shown in Row 4 or 5. By the same token, many knife collectors are missing the "Stonex" knife shown on Row 5.

So, keep in mind that not everyone collects Kitchenware by color. Many collect by items. Therefore, the competition is intensified!

Row	#	Item	Price
Row 1:	#1	Embossed "Coffee" canister	65.00– 75.00
	#2	Embossed "Tea" canister	55.00– 65.00
	#3-6	Spice shakers, ea.	22.00– 25.00
	#7	Salt box	125.00–150.00
	#8	Measuring cup	150.00–175.00
Row 2:	#1	Sugar canister	85.00–100.00
	#2	New Martinsville batter set	100.00–125.00
	#3	Cambridge etched grapes design ice bucket	35.00– 40.00
	#4	Valencia reamer, unembossed	175.00–225.00
Row 3:	#1	Water bottle	45.00– 55.00
	#2-5	U.S. Glass mixing bowl set (4)	80.00–100.00
		9" bowl	30.00– 35.00
		8" bowl	20.00– 25.00
		7" bowl	17.50– 22.50
		6" bowl	15.00– 17.50
Row 4:	#1	Cake stand (fairly recent vintage)	15.00– 17.50
	#2	Fry reamer	300.00–325.00
	#3	Butter dish (foreign)	40.00– 50.00
	#4	Butter dish (similar to canisters above)	50.00– 60.00
Row 5:	#1	Indiana Glass reamer	200.00–250.00
	#2	Fry oval tray	35.00– 45.00
	#3	Knife, 8¼", "Stonex"	90.00– 110.00
	#4	Knife rest	17.50– 20.00
	#5	Apothecary measure, 1 oz.	25.00– 30.00

AMBER (Continued)

It seems that the more avid collectors of amber buy the darker shades; however, to have a useable set, you need to consider that amber color intensities vary greatly as is illustrated by our pictures. One shade of amber is nearly impossible to gather together.

It took three years to find enough new items to make this fourth book possible – and we photographed collections from three states: California, Ohio and Kentucky.

I was particularly interested in getting west coast price input!

One note regarding the drawer pulls on Row 5. Drawer pulls with small screws are still more in demand than those with large screws ostensibly because smaller screws do not damage furniture as badly.

Row 1:	#1	Chesterfield pitcher	65.00– 75.00
	#2	Chesterfield mug	20.00– 22.50
	#3	Imperial syrup	55.00– 65.00
	#4	Sugar shaker	110.00–135.00
	#5	"Visible" mail box	60.00– 75.00
Row 2:	#1	Cambridge oval covered casserole	22.50– 25.00
	#2	Cambridge covered casserole with underliner	20.00– 22.50
	#3	Cheese dish (possibly foreign)	50.00– 60.00
Row 3:	#1	U.S. Glass 2 cup and reamer top	250.00–300.00
	#2	Cambridge 2-spouted gravy boat	17.50– 20.00
	#3	Cambridge footed cream sauce boat for asparagus platter	20.00– 22.50
	#4	Westmoreland 2-piece reamer	150.00–200.00
	#5	Lemon reamer (foreign)	85.00–100.00
	#6	Oil bottle	22.00– 25.00
Row 4:	#1	Paden City "Party Line" ice bucket	25.00– 27.50
	#2	Same, 14 oz. tumbler	8.00– 10.00
	#3	Paden City egg cup	8.00– 10.00
	#4	Paden City hotel sugar and cover	20.00– 25.00
	#5	Paden City salt box	85.00–100.00
	#6	Cambridge oil bottle	35.00– 40.00
	#7	Tobacco jar	22.00– 25.00
Row 5:	#1	"Feathered" curtain tie backs, pr.	20.00– 22.50
	#2	"Sandwich" round tie backs, pr.	20.00– 25.00
	#3	"Plume" tie backs or small round, pr.	17.50– 20.00
	#4	et. al. drawer pulls, ea. (large screws)	5.00– 7.00
		Same w/small screws	10.00– 12.50
	#5	Door knobs, set	60.00– 75.00

AMBER and BLACK

The shade of amber most easily found is the lighter shade shown in lower half of the photo on page 11. There has been a reluctance on the part of new collectors to begin buying amber as a kitchen collectible; and because of this, there has been some price adjusting since the last book. Reamers, sugar shakers and unusual items are still in demand, but some of the more common pieces are difficult to sell. The Cambridge reamer (Row 3, #1) remains one of the prime amber collectibles; however, the measuring cups (Row 4, #3 and Row 5, #3) are examples of supply more than equaling demand.

Black still carries a mystique of its own for collectors. In fact, we experimented with using it for a cover photo, but Delphite won out. The five reamers shown on page 13 are all prizes worthy of finding. They each will play havoc with the glass budget, unless you have a deep pocket!

Amber
Page 11

Row 1:	#1	Cocktail shaker	60.00– 65.00
	#2-4	Jars (recent vintage)	15.00– 20.00
	#5	Tobacco jar	20.00– 22.50
	#6	Sugar shaker	40.00– 45.00
Row 2:	#1	Batter jug, Paden City	40.00– 45.00
	#2	Tobacco jar	20.00– 22.50
	#3	Sugar shaker, Paden City	125.00–150.00
	#4	Sugar shaker	115.00–135.00
	#5	Sugar shaker	50.00– 60.00
	#6	Syrup, Cambridge	40.00– 50.00
Row 3:	#1	Reamer, Cambridge	600.00–700.00
	#2	Reamer, foreign	50.00– 60.00
	#3	Reamer, top only	50.00– 60.00
		Same, complete	150.00–175.00

Row 3:	(Continued)		
	#4	Sugar Shaker, Paden City	125.00–150.00
	#5	Syrup	40.00– 50.00
Row 4:	#1	Reamer, Westmoreland	200.00–250.00
	#2	Butter, ¼ lb., Federal	22.00– 25.00
	#3	Measure cup, no handle	32.00– 35.00
	#4	Butter, ¼ lb., Federal	22.00– 25.00
	#5	Jelly jar	12.00– 15.00
Row 5:	**All Federal Glass Company**		
	#1	Butter, 1 lb.	25.00– 30.00
	#2	Butter tub	22.00– 25.00
	#3	Measure cup, w/handle	35.00– 38.00
	#4	Reamer, tab handle	10.00– 12.50
	#5	Reamer, tab handle	275.00–300.00

Black
Page 12

Row 1:	#1	Sellers sugar canister	60.00– 70.00
	#2	Salt or pepper, ea.	12.00– 15.00
	#3	McKee batter jug	60.00– 65.00
	#4	Cocktail shaker	30.00– 40.00
	#5	Syrup, covered, Fenton	40.00– 50.00
Row 2:	#1	McKee, 4½" salt (harder to find than pepper)	12.00– 15.00
		Same, pepper (weak lettering–50% of prices)	8.00– 10.00
		Same, flour or sugar	12.00– 15.00
	#2	McKee, 3½" sugar (priced as above)	12.00– 15.00
	#3	Covered ice bucket	60.00–70.00
	#4	McKee tumbler	15.00– 18.00
	#5	Straw in tumbler	4.00– 5.00
	#6	Paden City batter jug set	175.00–200.00

Row 3:		All shakers priced as in Row 2 with those having badly worn or missing lettering 50% of prices listed) EXCEPT last pr.	35.00– 40.00
Row 4:	#1	Butter dish w/crystal top (possibly foreign)	50.00– 65.00
	#2	Egg cup	10.00– 12.50
	#3	Drawer pull, double	12.00– 15.00
	#4	Paden City, "Party Line" napkin holder	115.00–135.00
	#5	Nar-O-Fold Napkin Company Chicago, U.S.A.	115.00–135.00
Row 5:	#1	Punch ladle	50.00– 60.00
	#2-5	Drawer pulls, ea.	8.00– 10.00
	#3	Cambridge salad set	85.00–100.00

Page 13

Row 1:	#1	Cookie jar, L. E. Smith	50.00– 60.00
	#2	Batter jug, Fenton	100.00– 125.00
	#3	Syrup, same	40.00– 50.00
	#4	Reamer pitcher, Fenton	800.00–1,000.00
Row 2:	#1	Ice bucket	50.00– 60.00
	#2	Jar, import?	15.00– 20.00
	#3	Sugar shaker	225.00– 250.00
	#4	Saunders reamer	750.00– 850.00
Row 3:	#1	McKee grapefruit reamer	750.00– 850.00
	#2	Sunkist reamer	400.00– 450.00
	#3-5	Shakers, ea.	12.50– 15.00
	#6	Tray for batter set	25.00– 30.00

Row 4:	#1	Mixing bowl, 9⅜"	35.00– 40.00
		Bowl, 8⅜" (not shown)	32.50– 35.00
		Bowl, 7⅜" (not shown)	30.00– 32.50
		Bowl, 6⅜" (not shown)	22.50– 25.00
		Bowl, 5⅜" (not shown)	18.00– 20.00
	#2	Bowl, 7⅜" McKee	25.00– 30.00
	#3	Mug	22.00– 25.00
	#4	Ladle	25.00– 30.00
Row 5:	#1	McKee, 2 spout	500.00– 550.00
	#2	Reamer, Tricia	800.00–1,000.00
	#3	Tray	25.00– 30.00
	#4	Shaker, Fenton hobnail	25.00– 30.00

BLUE (Chalaine) and PEACOCK BLUE

Those of you who think you are having a difficult time collecting another color in Kitchenware ought to try these! On second thought, please forget I said that, as we have only added four or five pieces to our Chalaine blue collection in the last few years. I do not need any more competition!

Although there seems to be even less Peacock Blue available than Chalaine, I've seen pictures of lovely and fairly extensive collections of this color. Therefore, it is not totally impossible to collect.

Chalaine Blue
Page 15

Row 1: #1-4 Canisters (press-on lids),
ea. 175.00–200.00
#5 Refrigerator dish, 4" x 5"
(shown stacked) ea. 35.00– 45.00
Row 2: #1-4 Shakers, ea. 30.00– 35.00
#5 Shaker, nutmeg 45.00– 50.00
#6 Sunkist reamer 145.00–165.00
Row 3: #1 Butter dish, plain, no
tabs 250.00-300.00
#2 Butter dish, ribbed, tab
handles 225.00–250.00

Row 3: (Continued)
#3 Ginger (?) jar 25.00– 30.00
Row 4: #1 Measure pitcher, 4 cup 150.00–175.00
#2 Measure cup, 2 spout 500.00–550.00
#3 Rolling pin, shaker top 350.00–400.00
Row 5: #1 Refrigerator dish, 7¼" sq. 85.00– 95.00
#2 Toothbrush holder 20.00– 25.00
#3 Towel bar, 17" 30.00– 35.00
#4 Drawer pull, double 12.00– 15.00
#5 Drawer pull, single 8.00– 10.00

Page 16

Row 1: #1 Pitcher, ftd. (possibly
Fenton) 150.00–175.00
#2 Measure pitcher, 4 cup 500.00–600.00
#3-5 Canisters, screw-on lids
175.00–200.00
Row 2: #1 Canister, rnd., 48 oz.,
blue lid 55.00– 65.00
#2 Canister, rnd., 24 oz.,
blue lid 35.00– 40.00
#3 Canister, rnd., 10 oz.,
blue lid 35.00– 40.00
Row 3: #1 Beater bowl, w/spout,
4½" tall 30.00– 35.00

Row 3: (Continued)
#2 Beater bowl, w/spout,
4" tall 30.00– 35.00
#3 Grapefruit reamer 350.00–450.00
#4 Egg cup 12.00– 15.00
Row 4: #1 Mixing bowl, 9" 50.00– 60.00
#2 Bowl, 7½" 35.00– 45.00
#3 Bowl, 6" 25.00– 30.00
Row 5: #1, 2 Salt box (2 shades) 150.00–175.00
#3 Shakers, (2 shades)
embossed print (flour
$60.00-65.00) others 70.00– 75.00

Peacock Blue
Page 17

Row 1: #1 Strawholder (probably
1950's) 150.00–200.00
#2 L.E. Smith cookie jar 60.00– 75.00
#3 Imperial decanter 25.00– 27.50
#4 Dispenser (for a liquid
or syrup) 100.00–125.00
Row 2: #1 Sugar, 5 lb. canister 175.00–200.00
#2 Canister, 40 oz. canister 95.00–110.00
#3 Tea, 20 oz. canister 85.00– 95.00
#4-6 Shakers, 8 oz., ea. 40.00– 50.00
#7 Salt box 125.00–150.00
Row 3: #1 Ice tub 20.00– 25.00
#2 Rolling pin 150.00–200.00

Row 3: (Continued)
#3 Mug 25.00–30.00
Row 4: #1 Jar (paper label, sold
by route merchants) 10.00–12.50
#2-8 Tie backs, large pr. 25.00–30.00
small pr. 20.00–25.00
Row 5: #1, 3 Towel rods, ea. 25.00–27.50
#2 Double towel rod 30.00–35.00
Row 6: #1, 2 Spoons, ea. 15.00–22.50
#3, 4 Salad set 55.00–70.00
#5, 6 Double drawer pulls, ea. 18.00–20.00
#7-11 Single drawer pulls, ea. 10.00–12.00

14

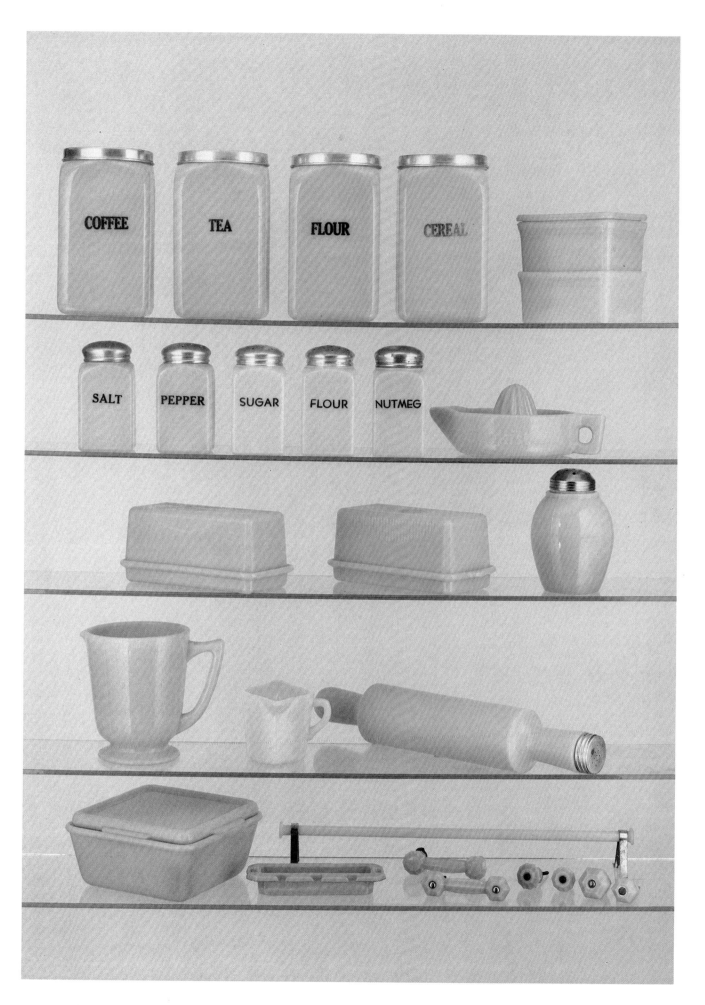

BLUE (Cobalt)

Cobalt blue ware has a special allure for many collectors. Be it kitchenware, dinnerware or decorative pieces, even non-collectors are attracted to it. Cobalt blue canisters with nice lettering and undamaged lids are bringing big prices. There are quite a few canisters with worn lettering and chipped lids available, but collectors are willing to pay a premium for mint canisters.

Those items with an asterisk (*) in the book have been reproduced! See pages 221-223 for further information. On page 19, Row 2, #1 and #5 have both been reproduced and the price has made a downward adjustment for the present time. It will probably only be temporary!

Page 19   All Hazel Atlas except last row.

Row 1: #1-5 Canister w/lid (deduct
          75.00-100.00 for worn
          lettering)   250.00–300.00
Row 2: #1 2-Cup measure w/reamer
          top   *200.00–250.00
       #2 Tab-handled orange
          reamer   225.00–250.00
       #3 Tab-handled lemon
          reamer   250.00–300.00
       #4 Milk pitcher   50.00– 60.00
       #5 1-Cup measure, 3
          spout   *250.00–300.00
Row 3: #1 Stack refrigerator,
          4½" x 5", ea.   40.00– 45.00
       #2 Round refrigerator, 5¾"   50.00– 60.00
       #3 Water bottle, 64 oz.,
          10" tall   55.00– 60.00

Row 3: (Continued)
       #4 Hazel Atlas bottle, (possibly
          medicinal)   20.00– 25.00
       #5 Mixer, Vidrio Products   110.00–125.00
Row 4: #1 Butter dish   150.00–165.00
       #2 Bowl, 5¾", "Restwell"   15.00– 17.50
       #3 Bowl, 6"   15.00– 17.50
       #4 Tumbler, marked HA   10.00– 15.00
Row 5: #1 Spoon stirrer   8.00– 10.00
       #2 Curtain tie back   15.00– 17.50
       #3 Drawer pull   10.00– 12.00
       #4, 5 Stirrers, ea.   1.00– 1.50
       #6-8 Spoons or forks, ea.   27.50– 35.00
       #9 Coaster   5.00– 7.50

Page 20

Row 1: #1 Bowl, 8½" (add $5.00
          w/metal)   22.50–25.00
       #2 Bowl, 7⅝" (add $5.00
          w/metal)   20.00–22.50
       #3 Bowl, 6⅝" (add $5.00
          w/metal)   15.00–17.50
Row 2: #1 Bowl, 9⅝" (add $5.00
          w/metal)   30.00–32.50
       #2 Bowl, 10⅝"   45.00–50.00
       #3 Bowl, 11⅝" (all of above
          are Hazel Atlas)   55.00–65.00

Row 3: #1 L.E. Smith water
          dispenser   300.00–350.00
       #2 Cambridge mug   35.00– 50.00
       #3 Shakers, pr. (possibly
          bath powder)   18.00– 20.00
Row 4: #1 L.E. Smith bowl, 8¼"   40.00– 42.50
       #2 Same, 7¼"   35.00– 37.50
       #3 Same, 6¼"   30.00– 32.50
Row 5: #1 Mustard pot   20.00– 25.00
       #2 Fry cake plate, 3 ftd.   75.00– 85.00
       #3, 4 Fork and spoon, set   45.00– 55.00

Page 21

Row 1: #1 Barbell cocktail shaker   75.00– 85.00
       #2 Strawholder   250.00–275.00
       #3 Cocktail shaker   35.00– 40.00
       #4 McKee batter jug   70.00– 80.00
Row 2: #1 New Martinsville batter
          set   250.00–275.00
       #2, 3 Shakers w/blue tops   25.00– 35.00
       #4 Sugar shaker (older than
          Depression era)   150.00– 175.00
       #5 Sugar shaker   300.00– 350.00

Row 2: (Continued)
       #6 Tumble up   35.00– 40.00
Row 3: #1 Paden City batter jug   40.00– 45.00
       #2 Same, milk jug   35.00– 40.00
       #3 Same, syrup jug   30.00– 35.00
       #4 Cambridge reamer   2,000.00–2,500.00
Row 4: #1 Cobalt rolling pin   300.00– 350.00
       #2 Cobalt handles rolling
          pin   175.00– 200.00

BLUE (Delphite) Jeannette Glass Co., Late '30's

Delphite continues to be one of the most desirable colors of Kitchen collectibles. Certain Jeannette round canisters are becoming impossible to find at any price. The coffee canister remains the easiest of the larger canisters to find, but many collectors have never located the sugar. While you may find the smaller round shakers, especially the salt and pepper, there is a scarcity of the square shakers as found in Row 4. Next to the square shakers is a one-cup measure without a spout. Someone has ground off a badly chipped spout!

Shown for the first time is the large-size Delphite reamer in Row 3, #1 with the more commonly found smaller reamer beside it for comparison. All drippings jars are not found with black lettering. The price without the lettering is only half (or less) of the price shown below.

I wish you luck in your search for this color. Usually a color that is featured on the cover may experience some price escalation. So be forewarned!

Row 1:	#1	Canister, 40 oz., sugar	135.00–	150.00
	#2	Same, coffee	115.00–	135.00
	#3	Canister, 20 oz., tea	85.00–	95.00
	#4	Shaker, 8 oz., paprika	40.00–	45.00
	#5	Same, sugar	35.00–	40.00
		Same, flour	35.00–	40.00
	#6	Matches holder	40.00–	45.00
	#7	Bowl w/metal beater	45.00–	50.00
Row 2:	#1	Bowl, 5½", horizontal rib	25.00–	30.00
	#2	Measure, 1 cup	40.00–	42.50
		Same, ½ cup	32.00–	35.00
		Same, ⅓ cup	25.00–	30.00
		Same, ¼ cup	20.00–	25.00
	#3	Bowl, 7½", horizontal rib	35.00–	40.00
	#4	Bowl, 9¾", horizontal rib	55.00–	65.00
		Bowl set #1, 3, 4	115.00–	135.00
Row 3:	#1	Reamer, large	900.00–	1,000.00
	#2	Reamer, small	55.00–	65.00
	#3, 5	Shaker, salt or pepper	18.00–	20.00
	#4	Drippings jar w/lettering	50.00–	55.00
Row 4:	#1	2-cup pitcher sunflower bottom	40.00–	45.00
	#2	Butter	145.00–	155.00
	#3	Cup measure (spout removed)	25.00–	30.00
	#4, 5	Shaker, square salt or pepper	40.00–	45.00
	#6, 7	Same, flour or sugar	55.00–	60.00
Row 5:	#1-3	Canister, square, 29 oz., 5", ea.	75.00–	85.00
	#4, 5	Mixing bowl set (4) vertical rib	100.00–	120.00
		Bowl, 6", rare	25.00–	30.00
		Bowl, 7"	20.00–	25.00
		Bowl, 8"	25.00–	30.00
		Bowl, 9"	30.00–	35.00

BLUE DELPHITE and BLUE MISCELLANEOUS

There are a few new pieces of McKee Delphite scattered throughout this book. Below is one of the more important finds. In the center is the first known McKee screw-lid canister.

On the left is the first known Delphite top to the commonly found Jeannette 2-cup measure pitcher which has the Sunflower design in the bottom. On the right is an electric beater which has been turned for better visibility.

Page 24

	#1	Reamer pitcher	1,000.00–1,200.00
	#2	Canister, 48 oz.	100.00– 125.00
	#3	Electric beater	40.00– 45.00

Page 25

Row 1:
#1	McKee measure pitcher, 4 cup	400.00– 450.00
#2	McKee measure pitcher, 2 cup	55.00– 75.00
#3	McKee 48 oz. round canister	55.00– 65.00
#4	McKee 10 oz. round canister	35.00– 40.00
#5	Vase	25.00– 28.00
#6	Ginger (?) jar	15.00– 18.00

Row 2:
#1	McKee butter dish	155.00– 170.00
#2	McKee refrigerator dish, 4" x 5"	22.50– 25.00
#3, 4	Shakers, ea.	45.00– 50.00
#5	Ash tray, possibly McKee or Pyrex	12.00– 15.00

Row 3:
#1	Mixing bowl, 9"	30.00– 40.00
#2	Mixing bowl, 7⅜"	25.00– 30.00
#3	Bowl w/spout, 4¼"	20.00– 25.00
#4	Bowl, 4⅜" (cocotte)	12.50– 15.00

Row 4:
#1	L.E. Smith, 9¼" bowl	50.00– 60.00
#2	L.E. Smith, 7" bowl	35.00– 40.00
#3	Fry, cornflower blue reamer	1,250.00–1,500.00
#4	Hocking, "Block Optic" butter dish	375.00– 425.00

Row 5:
#1	Cheese dish (possibly foreign)	80.00– 95.00
#2	Scoop	45.00– 50.00
#3	Paden City bunny, cotton ball dispenser	50.00– 60.00
#4	Soap dish, "Home Soap Company"	22.50– 25.00

"CLAMBROTH" WHITE and CRYSTAL

The translucent, washed-out white color shown in Rows 2, 3 and 4 on page 27 is commonly called "Clambroth" (white) by collectors. There is very little being offered on the market in this color (except for the rolling pin), but there is not a lot of demand for "Clambroth" white either. The most notable exception to that statement is the oval Pyrex casserole pictured in the middle of Row 3. This casserole is embossed "Pyrex" on one end and "193-197" on the other. To date, this is the only one of these to surface! There are several reamers shown in "Clambroth" white in that section.

Crystal kitchenware is still available at fairly reasonable prices when compared to many of the popular colored wares. However, the demand for any kitchen collectible is beginning to deplete even this supply. Remember, I warned you to take heed, and collect NOW!

On page 29, Row 4 #1 is an item marked, "The Pot Watcher." My understanding is that this is placed in the bottom of a pan or pot, and when the pot begins to boil, this glass piece begins to rattle around announcing that the pot is boiling.

Page 27
Row 1:	#1	Canister, Owens-Illinois, frosted, 40 oz.	12.50–15.00
	#2, 3	Same, 20 oz.	10.00–12.50
	#4, 5	Cruet, frosted, chicken decal, ea.	10.00–12.00
Row 2:	#1	Rolling pin w/wooden handles	75.00–85.00
	#2	Sugar shaker, lid w/one hole	35.00–40.00
	#3, 4	Salt or pepper w/normal lid	12.00–15.00
Row 3:	#1	Canister, large	25.00–27.50
	#2	Pyrex oval casserole	75.00–95.00
	#3	Canister, medium	22.50–25.00
		wo/label subtract $5.00 on canisters	
Row 4:	#1	Tray, 10⅝", square	15.00–20.00
	#2	Server, 7⅜", round	10.00–12.00
	#3	Server, 9⅞", round	15.00–18.00

Page 28
Row 1:	#1	Canister, large, w/"Taverne" scene	20.00–22.50
	#2	Canister, medium, same	18.00–20.00
	#3, 4	Shaker, ovoid shape, Owens–Illinois, ea.	6.00– 7.50
	#5	Canister, ovoid shape, Owens-Illinois	15.00–18.00
Row 2:	#1	Instant coffee, w/sterling top	25.00–30.00
	#2	"Bohner's Safety crushed fruit bowl" (pat. Feb 22, 1898)	20.00–25.00
	#3-7	Sneath spice shaker, ea.	10.00–12.50
Row 3:	#1	Fleur-de-lis flour canister	10.00–12.00
	#2-4	Canister, 20 oz. ea.	8.00–10.00
	#5	8 oz. Kroger Embassy peanut butter	8.00–10.00
	#6	Spee-Dee mixer	20.00–25.00
Row 4:	#1-6	Small canister, 16 oz., ea.	6.00– 7.50
	#7	MOXIE (licensed only for serving)	20.00–25.00

Page 29
Row 1:	#1	Canister, Dutch boy design	15.00–20.00
	#2	Canister, embossed coffee	15.00–18.00
	#3	Canister, emb. coffee, Zipper design	18.00-20.00
	#4	"Kwik Whip all purpose mixer"	8.00–10.00
	#5	"No Drip Server," Federal Tool Corp., 1 qt.	6.00– 7.50
Row 2:	#1	Salt, large	20.00–25.00
	#2	Salt, small	20.00–25.00
	#3	Canister, embossed tea	12.50–15.00
	#4	Syrup, w/glass top (2 pc.)	20.00–25.00
	#5	Pint server (same as #5 in *Row 1*)	3.00– 3.50
Row 3:	#1, 6	Glasbake tea kettle, ea.	15.00–18.00
	#2	Canister, raised dots design	12.50–15.00
	#3-5	Shaker, raised dot design, ea.	5.00– 6.00
Row 4:	#1	"The Pot Watcher"	8.00–10.00
	#2	McKee Range Tec skillet	7.50– 9.00
	#3-8	Six-piece set from box marked "Serve U Set" Medco No 86 (A Complete Set of Table Servers for the Modern Hostess)	20.00–25.00

CRYSTAL

Crystal kitchenware lends itself to any kitchen decor. Most of it is reasonably priced, and it was made to be used, unlike many of today's products that are made to be disposed of after one use. The McKee water dispenser shown below has a separate center holder for the ice. I guess that idea never caught on, but it seems like a neat idea to me! The cooler below sells for $65.00–75.00.

Row 1:	#1	McKee Glasbake Scientific Measuring Cup	18.00–20.00
	#2-5	Hocking canister w/Dutch decal	15.00–20.00
	#6	Pint measure in tablespoons for coffee, tea & wine	18.00–20.00
Row 2:	#1, 2	John Alden (salt) & Priscilla (pepper), pr.	17.50–20.00
	#3	Westmoreland baby reamer, w/decal	35.00–40.00
	#4	Horseradish jar	10.00–12.50
	#5	Salt box	15.00–17.50
	#6	Toast holder	45.00–50.00
	#7	Spoon holder (Pat. Feb. 11, 1913)	15.00–18.00
Row 3:	#1-8	Dutch shakers (12 oz.), ea. (Cocoa in 6th)	8.00– 9.00
	#9-10	Dutch shakers (16 oz.)	10.00–12.00
Row 4:	#1	Flour canister, 128 oz.	30.00–35.00
	#2	Coffee dripolator	10.00–12.50
	#3	Measure spoon (markings for table, dessert, tea)	4.00– 5.00
	#4	Sprinkler (leaning in back) cardboard wrapped instructions	17.50–20.00
	#5	Cambridge ash tray holder	30.00–35.00
	#6	Jiffy one-cup coffee maker w/filter	8.00–10.00

CUSTARD and CARAMEL, McKee Glass Company

The darker shade of Custard (shown in the bottom row on page 33), is referred to as caramel by collectors. The five pieces shown here are all difficult to find, and this is the largest group of caramel pieces I have ever seen at one time! The canister on the far right is not a fired-on color, but a solid caramel color like the other pieces. I mention that because I have seen a few fired-on pieces similar in color.

Custard is still readily available, but its popularity with collectors leaves a lot to be desired. There are some elusive items, however. If you would like a challenge, try to put together a set of the lady with apron shakers or try to match a set of four (salt, pepper, flour, sugar) in one particular lettering design. Unless you buy a complete set at one time, it will take a lot of searching to come up with a matching set.

Although the Sunkist custard reamer is abundant, custard grapefruit reamers are few and far between.

Page 33

Row 1:	#1, 2	Canister, coffee or tea, ea.	40.00– 50.00
	#3	Measure pitcher, 4 cup	25.00– 30.00
	#4	Bowl, 9"	18.00– 20.00
Row 2:	#1	Bowl, 8"	15.00– 18.00
		Bowl, 7" (not shown)	12.00– 15.00
	#2	Bowl, 6"	10.00– 12.00
	#3, 4	Shaker, Roman arch, flour, sugar	12.00– 15.00
	#5, 6	Same, salt or pepper	10.00– 12.00
Row 3:	#1-4	Salt or pepper shakers, ea.	10.00– 12.00
	#5	Cinnamon shaker	20.00– 22.00
	#6-9	Flour or sugar shaker, ea.	14.00– 16.00
Row 4:	#1	Pepper shaker	12.00– 14.00
	#2	Lady w/apron shaker	15.00– 17.50
	#3	Custard or jello	4.00– 5.00
	#4	Pitcher, 2 cup	15.00– 18.00
	#5	Tumbler	8.00– 10.00
	#6	Tom & Jerry mug	10.00– 12.00
Row 5:	#1	Reamer, 6" embossed McK	30.00– 35.00
	#2	Grapefruit reamer	300.00–350.00
	#3	Sunkist reamer	25.00– 30.00
Row 6:	**All Caramel Color**		
	#1	Canister, 40 oz.	65.00– 75.00
	#2	Grapefruit reamer	650.00–750.00
	#3	Sunkist reamer	250.00–300.00
	#4	Measure cup, 2 spout	400.00–500.00
	#5	Canister, 48 oz	75.00– 85.00

33

FOREST GREEN

Page 35

Row 1: #1 Owens-Illinois vinegar or water
bottle w/tray 30.00–35.00
Same w/o tray 10.00–12.50
#2 Hocking water bottle w/top 22.50–25.00
#3 Duraglas water bottle 20.00–25.00
#4 McKee syrup (goes with #5) 30.00–35.00
#5 Oil & Vinegar set (goes w/#4) 20.00–25.00

Row 2: #1, 2 Owens-Illinois canisters (ovoid
shape), ea. 25.00–27.50
Same, medium size TEA, RICE
(not shown) 18.00–20.00
#3 Same, shaker size 9.00–10.00
Prices for #1, 2, 3 (30% to
40% less w/missing lettering)
#4 Owens-Illinois embossed COFFEE
w/flip top 40.00–45.00

Row 2: (Continued)
#5 Owens-Illinois water bottle 12.50– 15.00
Row 3: #1-3 Owens-Illinois 40 oz. diagonal
ridged canister, ea. 17.50– 20.00
#4-5 Same, 20 oz., ea (TEA, RICE) 14.00– 16.00
#6 Same, 10 oz. 7.50– 8.50
#7, 8 Shakers, ea. 6.00– 8.00
Row 4: #1 New Martinsville batter jug 50.00– 55.00
#2 Same, syrup jug 40.00– 45.00
#3 Cruet 32.00– 35.00
#4 Sugar shaker (1950's) 60.00– 65.00
Row 5: #1, 2 Curtain rings, ea. 8.00– 10.00
#3 Rolling pin 125.00–150.00
#4, 5 Shakers, pr. 15.00– 17.50

GREEN "CLAMBROTH" etc.

Page 36

Row 1: #1-4 Hocking canisters w/glass
lid, 47 oz., ea. 35.00– 40.00
#5-8 Hocking shakers, 8 oz. ea. 15.00– 17.50
Row 2: #1 Hocking oval refrig. dish, 8" 30.00– 35.00
#2 Same, 7" 22.00– 25.00
#3 Same, 6" 15.00– 18.00
#4 Refrigerator jar, 4¼" x 4¾" 20.00– 22.50
#5 Hocking drippings jar (possibly
powder jar) 15.00– 20.00
#6 Hocking 2-cup measure 85.00–100.00
Row 3: #1 Hocking 1-cup measure 135.00–150.00
#2 Hocking reamer 90.00–115.00
#3 Fenton reamer top for
pitcher 75.00–100.00
#4 Jadite Sunkist (there is one
that is much more trans-
lucent than this) 18.00– 20.00

Row 3: (Continued)
#5 Cold cream jar 12.00– 15.00
#6 Mug 25.00– 30.00
Row 4: #1 Owl "tumble-up" ·nite set
(pitcher & glass as top) 85.00–100.00
#2 Butter dish 55.00– 65.00
#3 McKee Hall's refrigerator
dish, 4" x 6" 10.00– 14.00
#4 Water dispenser w/crystal top 45.00– 55.00
Row 5: #1 Ice bucket, Fenton 35.00– 40.00
#2 Whipped cream pail 30.00– 35.00
#3 Fenton pitcher missing lid
(as pictured) 40.00– 50.00
#4 Towel bar holders, pr. 20.00– 25.00
#5 Sugar shaker 25.00– 30.00
#6 "Serv-All" napkin holder 100.00–135.00

Page 37

Row 1: #1 Pitcher (Fenton?) 50.00–60.00
#2 Tumbler to match above 8.00–10.00
#3 Fenton ice bucket & lid 75.00–85.00
#4 Tumbler, ftd. 10.00–12.00
#5 Sherbert 6.00– 7.50
#6 Door knob set 35.00–45.00
Row 2: #1 Mixing bowl, 8¾" 15.00–20.00
#2 Same, 7¾" 12.00–15.00
#3 Same, 6¾" 10.00–12.00
#4 Powder shaker? 15.00–18.00
Row 3: #1 Ash tray 4.00– 5.00
#2 Wall tumbler holder 8.00–10.00
#3 Coaster 8.00–10.00
#4 Furniture "foot rest" (per 1920's
Montgomery Ward catalogue) 4.00– 5.00
#5 Jadite towel bar in rear 20.00–25.00

Row 3: (Continued)
#6 Soap dish 12.00– 15.00
#7 Jade ash tray 4.00– 5.00
#8 Jade makeup holder 12.00– 15.00
Row 4: #1, 2 Canisters, fired-on ea. 30.00– 35.00
#3 Decanter, pinched 85.00–100.00
#4 Water bottle 85.00–100.00
#5 Bowl, 4¾" twist design 10.00– 12.00
#6 McKee bottoms up w/coaster
(coaster $40.00-50.00) 70.00– 80.00
Row 5: #1 Jadite vinegar cruet 110.00–125.00
#2 Refrigerator dish, wedge
shaped 15.00– 20.00
#3 Refrigerator w/jade lid 8.00– 10.00
#4 Cigarette ash tray 12.00– 15.00
#5 Bowl, 4½" 8.00– 10.00

GREEN JADITE, JEANNETTE and McKEE COMPANIES,
(Called "SKOKIE GREEN" by McKee)

Jadite continues to be very popular with collectors. The price of many pieces remains reasonable despite heavy demand. Many items were produced abundantly and can still be found with searching. Other items, as can be seen by the price, are not so easily found. I believe the Saunders reamer pictured to be McKee, although there has been no documentation to support that yet!

Page 39 (Jeannette Glass Co.)

Row 1:	#1-4	Canister, square, 5½" high, 48 oz., ea.	30.00–32.00
		Same, Floral pattern inside lid	28.00–30.00
	#5	Beater bowl, w/beater	20.00–25.00
Row 2:	#1, 2	Jadite, light, salt or pepper	10.00–12.00
	#3, 4	Same, flour or sugar	12.00–15.00
	#5, 6	Jadite, dark, salt or pepper	12.00–14.00
	#7, 8	Same, flour or sugar	13.00–16.00
	#9	Butter, light	30.00–35.00
Row 3:	#1	Reamer, large, light	18.00–20.00
	#2	Same, dark	20.00–25.00
	#3	Refrigerator dish, 5" x 5" (Floral lid)	18.00–20.00
	#4	Butter, dark	35.00–38.00
Row 4:	#1-4	Canister, square, 29 oz., ea.	28.00–30.00
	#5	Refrigerator dish, 10" x 5", (Floral lid)	28.00–30.00

Row 5:	#1-4	Spice canister, 3", ea.	30.00– 32.00
	#5	Child's size cannister "sugar" (others include coffee, cereal, tea)	45.00– 50.00
	#6	Refrigerator dish, 4" x 4"	11.00– 13.00
	#7	Same, 4" x 8"	15.00– 18.00
Row 6:	#1	Batter jug (bottom only - $50.00)	150.00–200.00
	#2	Salt box	175.00–195.00
	#3	Reamer pitcher, 2 cup, light	15.00– 20.00
	#4	Same, dark (price varies as top & bottom match correctly)	60.00–100.00

Page 40 (Jeannette Glass Co.)

Row 1:	#1, 2	Canister, round, screw-on lid, 40 oz. coffee, light or dark	35.00–40.00
	#3	Same, sugar	40.00–45.00
	#4, 5	Same, 16 oz., tea	25.00–30.00
	#6	Vase	10.00–12.00
Row 2:	#1, 3	Salt or pepper	8.00–10.00
	#2	Drippings (no lettering - $20.00)	32.00–35.00
	#4, 5	Flour or sugar	10.00–12.00
	#6, 7	Decorated salt or pepper	13.00–15.00
	#8-10	Bicarbonate soda or mouth wash	30.00–35.00
Row 3:	#1	Round crock, 40 oz., knob on top	38.00–40.00
	#2	Tumbler, 12 oz.	10.00–12.00
	#3	Sugar shaker, dark	50.00–60.00
	#4	Sugar shaker, light	45.00–55.00

Row 3:	(Continued)		
	#5	Round refrigerator dish, 32 oz.	22.00–25.00
Row 4:	#1	Bowl, 5½", horizontal rib	10.00–12.00
	#2	Bowl, 8", vertical rib	12.00–15.00
	#3	Same, 7"	10.00–12.00
	#4	Same, 6"	8.00–10.00
		Same, 9" (not shown)	15.00–18.00
Row 5:	#1	Match holder (lettering $22.00-25.00)	10.00–12.00
	#2	Ash tray	6.00– 8.00
	#3	Reamer, small, light	20.00–22.00
	#4	Same, dark	22.00–25.00
Row 6:	#1	Bowl, 9¾", horizontal rib	20.00–25.00
	#2	Same, 7½"	12.00–15.00
	#3	Bowl, 9¾", vertical rib	15.00–18.00

Page 41 (McKee Glass Co.)

Row 1:	#1-4	Canister, 48 oz., screw-on lid, ea.	40.00– 50.00
	#5	Bottoms down mug	125.00–135.00
	#6	Pitcher, 4 cup	25.00– 30.00
Row 2:	#1	Reamer, large	18.00– 20.00
	#2	Reamer, small	18.00– 20.00
	#3	Refrigerator dish, 4" x 5"	10.00– 12.00
	#4	Pitcher, 2 cup	12.00– 15.00
Row 3:	#1	Bowl, 9"	15.00– 18.00
		Same, 8" (not shown)	12.00– 15.00
		Same, 7" (not shown)	10.00– 12.00
		Same, 6" (not shown)	8.00– 10.00
	#2	Marked 'McK' pat. pend. (any ideas?)	10.00– 12.00
	#3	"Roman" arch side panel, salt	20.00– 22.50
	#5, 7	Same, cinnamon or spice	30.00– 35.00
	#4, 6, 8	Same, pepper, flour or sugar	15.00– 18.00

Row 3:	(Continued)		
	#9	Tumbler or egg cup	8.00– 12.00
Row 4:	#1	"Tom & Jerry" bowl	65.00– 75.00
	#2	Measure cup, 2 spout	125.00–145.00
	#3	Baker, 5" x 3½", oval	10.00– 12.00
	#4	Grapefruit reamer	110.00–135.00
Row 5:	#1	"Tom & Jerry" mug	10.00– 12.00
	#2	Same, cup	8.00– 10.00
	#3	Egg beater bowl, w/spout	10.00– 12.00
	#4	Canister, round, 10 oz.	11.00– 13.00
		Same, 24 oz. (not shown)	15.00– 18.00
		Same, 40 oz. (not shown)	20.00– 22.50
	#5	Baker, 5" x 7", oval	12.00– 15.00
	#6	Custard cup	3.00– 5.00
Row 6:	#1	Measure pitcher, 4 cup, (sans handle)	175.00–225.00
	#2-5	Canister, 28 oz., square, ea.	35.00– 40.00
	#6	Saunders reamer	700.00–800.00

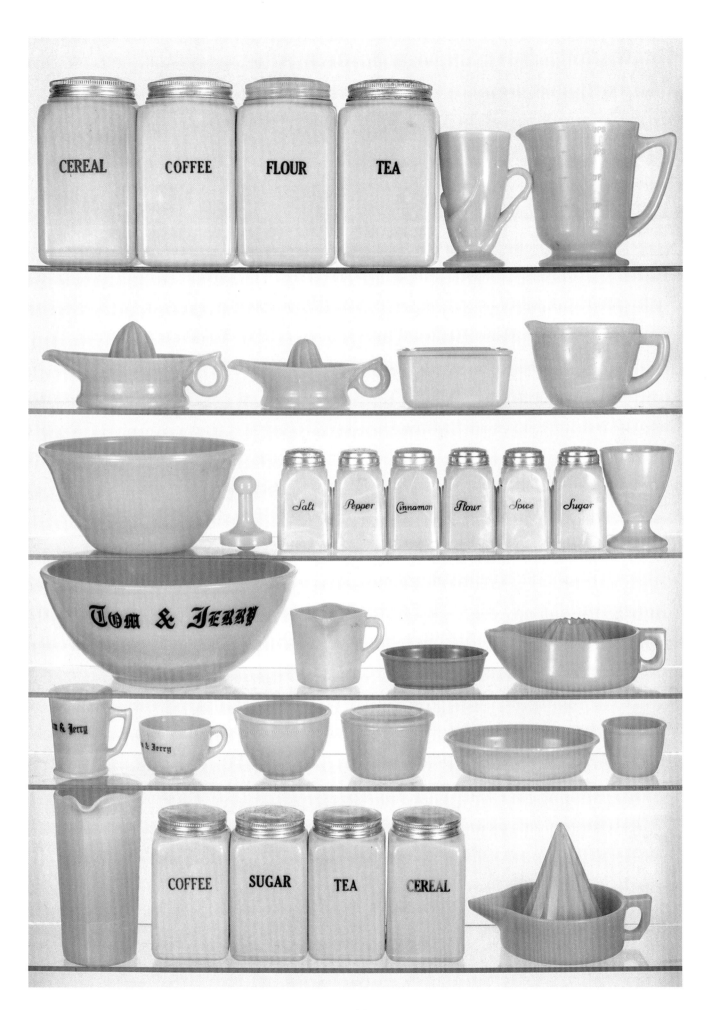

GREEN TRANSPARENT, JEANNETTE, HAZEL ATLAS, FEDERAL, and Others

I would like to point out the measuring pitcher on page 45, Row 1, #3 and Fenton's "Ming" pattern reamer on page 44, Row 3, #4 which is not shown in the reamer section of the book. Both of these items are desirable to collectors.

Page 43 All Jeannette Glass Co.

Row 1: #1 "Hex Optic" reamer
		bucket	35.00– 40.00
	#2	Beater bowl	18.00– 20.00
	#3	Cruet, w/correct stopper	75.00– 85.00
	#4	Jenkins batter jug	85.00–100.00

Row 2: #1 "Hex Optic" sugar
		shaker	125.00–145.00
	#2	Sugar shaker	40.00– 50.00
	#3	Sugar shaker	45.00– 55.00
	#4	Mug	22.50– 25.00
	#5	Measure cup, tab handle	25.00– 28.00
	#6	2-cup measure (Sunflower bottom)	75.00– 95.00

Row 3: #1 "Hex Optic" 4½" x 5"
| | | 'frige' jar | 18.00– 22.00 |

Row 3: (Continued)
	#2	Same, dark	18.00– 22.00
	#3	Same, butter	60.00– 65.00
	#4	"Floral," 5" x 5"	45.00– 55.00

Row 4: #1 Reamer, large — 15.00– 20.00
	#2	Tab reamer	12.50– 15.00
	#3	Reamer top (fits pitcher or bucket)	12.00– 15.00
	#4	Butter	32.50– 35.00

Row 5: #1 Covered 9" bowl — 35.00– 40.00
| | #2 | Salt box, 6", "SALT" on lid | 150.00–165.00 |
| | #3 | Butter, 2-lb. box | 100.00–125.00 |

Page 44

Row 1: #1 Paden City "Party Line"
| | | crushed fruit/cookie jar | 55.00– 65.00 |
| | #2-4 | Cambridge set etched #732 | 200.00–250.00 |

Row 2: #1 Stack sugar/creamer/plate — 40.00– 45.00
	#2, 3	Marmalade, ea.	20.00– 25.00
	#4	Stack set: Westmoreland sugar creamer/plate/shakers	50.00– 60.00
	#5, 6	Curtain tie back, ea.	8.00– 10.00
	#7	Ash tray	8.00– 10.00

Row 3: #1 Cambridge gravy & underliner — 45.00– 50.00
| | #2 | Bowl, 7¾" | 10.00– 12.50 |
| | #3 | Toothbrush holder, frosted | 12.50– 15.00 |

Row 3: (Continued)
| | #4 | Fenton "Ming" reamer | 450.00–500.00 |
| | #5 | Measure cup, 20 oz. | 125.00–150.00 |

Row 4: #1 Bottom to jar or canister — 20.00– 25.00
	#2	Kompakt dish units, 8" x 4" (Pat. June 16, 1925)	65.00– 75.00
	#3	Towel bar	25.00– 30.00
	#4, 5	Curtain tie backs, pr.	18.00– 20.00
	#6-8	Drawer pulls, ea. (large backs $4.00-5.00); small backs	7.00– 8.00
	#9	Double drawer pull	18.00– 20.00

Page 45

Row 1: #1 "Busy Betty" washing
		machine	200.00–250.00
	#2	Barrel cookie jar	40.00– 50.00
	#3	4-cup measure pitcher	250.00–300.00
	#4	Single doorknob	25.00– 30.00
	#5	Canister embossed COFFEE	100.00–110.00

Row 2: #1 Rolling pin — 275.00–325.00
| | #2 | "Zipper" canister embossed TEA | 85.00–100.00 |

Row 3: #1 Child's washboard embossed CRYSTAL — 150.00–200.00
| | #2 | Double towel bar | 30.00– 35.00 |
| | #3 | Double doorknob | 85.00–100.00 |

Row 4: #1, 5 Store shelf supports, ea. — 25.00– 35.00
	#2	Pickle jar	85.00–100.00
	#3	Door hook (screw-in type)	17.50– 20.00
	#4	Wall coffee dispenser	275.00–325.00

GREEN TRANSPARENT, U.S. GLASS, TUFGLASS and Others

On page 47 are a couple of interesting items. In Row 1, #6 is an item marked "ORASORB," which can also be found in an orchid color. If anyone knows the purpose of this, please let me know. In Row 5, #3 is a warming dish which has two containers for candles inside. These were placed on top to show them since they are difficult to see when inside the dish.

Page 47

Row 1:	#1	Canister, Hazel Atlas	40.00– 45.00
	#2	Canister, McKee (RARE)	55.00– 65.00
	#3, 4	Syrup, Hazel Atlas, ea.	20.00– 25.00
	#5	Syrup, Paden City	25.00– 30.00
	#6	"Orasorb" container	65.00– 75.00
Row 2:	#1, 2	Shaker, embossed salt or pepper	25.00– 30.00
	#3, 4	Same, embossed flour or sugar	45.00– 60.00
	#5	FAN FOLD napkin holder	85.00– 95.00
	#6	Measure cup, 3 spout, Federal	32.50– 35.00
	#7	Hazel Atlas tumbler	8.00– 10.00
	#8	Measure cup, Paden City	95.00–100.00
Row 3:	#1	Mixing bowl, 9"	16.00– 18.00
		Same, 8" (not shown)	12.50–15.00

Row 3:	(Continued)		
	#2	Same 7"	10.00–12.00
	#3	Same 6"	8.00–10.00
	#4	Same 5"	6.00– 7.50
Row 4:	#1	Butter, Hazel Atlas	35.00–40.00
	#2	Cheese plate ?	15.00–20.00
	#3	Measure cup (slightly oval)	40.00–50.00
	#4	Reamer top (scalloped edges)	45.00–50.00
Row 5:	#1	Fry tray 'Not heat resisting glass'	55.00–70.00
	#2	Lattice design refrigerator jar	15.00–18.00
	#3	Warming dish, two inserts	65.00–75.00

Page 48

Row 1:	#1	Sanitary jar	135.00–150.00
	#2	U.S. Glass reamer pitcher (snowflake in bottom)	50.00– 65.00
	#3	Slick-handled 9" covered bowl	35.00– 40.00
		w/o lid	15.00– 20.00
Row 2:	#1	Fluted sundae	15.00– 18.00
	#2	Soda	10.00– 12.00
	#3	Canning funnel	30.00– 35.00
	#4	Cruet	20.00– 25.00
	#5	Batter syrup (see page 81 R 3 # 2)	30.00– 35.00
	#6	U.S. Glass, 5" x 5"	12.50– 15.00

Row 3:	#1	Flask (hard day in kitchen!)	35.00– 45.00
	#2	"Tea Room" banana split	65.00– 75.00
	#3	Fluted sundae	20.00– 22.50
	#4	Cup, slick handle	8.00– 10.00
	#5	Banana split	20.00– 25.00
Row 4:	#1,3	Flat banana split, ea.	22.00– 27.00
	#2	9-oz. tumbler	8.00– 10.00
	#4	U.S. Glass covered dish	12.50– 15.00
Row 5:	#1,2	Salad set	60.00– 65.00
	#3	Spoon holder	150.00–175.00
	#4	Mug	20.00– 25.00

Tufglas
Page 49

Row 1:	#1	J.E. Marsden Glassworks mixing bowl, 5 pt., 10"	35.00– 40.00
	#2	Same, 3 pt., 9", made in Ambler, Pa.	30.00– 35.00
	#3	Same, 2 pt., 8", also not for oven use	25.00– 30.00
	#4	Same, 1½ pt., 7", for mixing, cooling & storing food	20.00– 25.00
Row 2:	#1	Butter dish	55.00– 65.00
	#2	Refrigerator dish, 3" x 6"	20.00– 25.00
	#3	Refrigerator dish, 6½" sq.	30.00– 35.00
	#4	"Tufglas Refrigerator Hydrator" No. 1	60.00– 65.00
Row 3:	#1	Tufglas tab-handled spouted bowl	25.00– 30.00
	#2	One-handled "No Splash Mixer"	30.00– 35.00
	#3	Measure pitcher, 36 oz.	75.00–100.00
	#4	Funnel	75.00– 85.00
	#5	Custard, "Trade Mark Tufglas Registered"	8.00– 10.00

Row 4:	#1	Reamer	60.00–75.00
	#2	Bowl, round, 4"	8.00–10.00
	#3	"Kold or Hot" small covered casserole	12.00–15.00
	#4	Jello mold	10.00–15.00
	#5	"Kold or Hot" Sanitary Food Mold	15.00–18.00
Row 5:	#1	4-cup "Kold or Hot" measure pitcher	30.00–35.00
	#2	Round refrigerator dish, "To seal, turn cover"	30.00–35.00
	#3	"Sanitary Butter Box," top only	30.00–35.00
	#4	Round bowl, wrinkled ridge, "Kold or Hot"	12.00–15.00
	#5	Custard w/ridges, "Kold or Hot"	2.00– 3.00

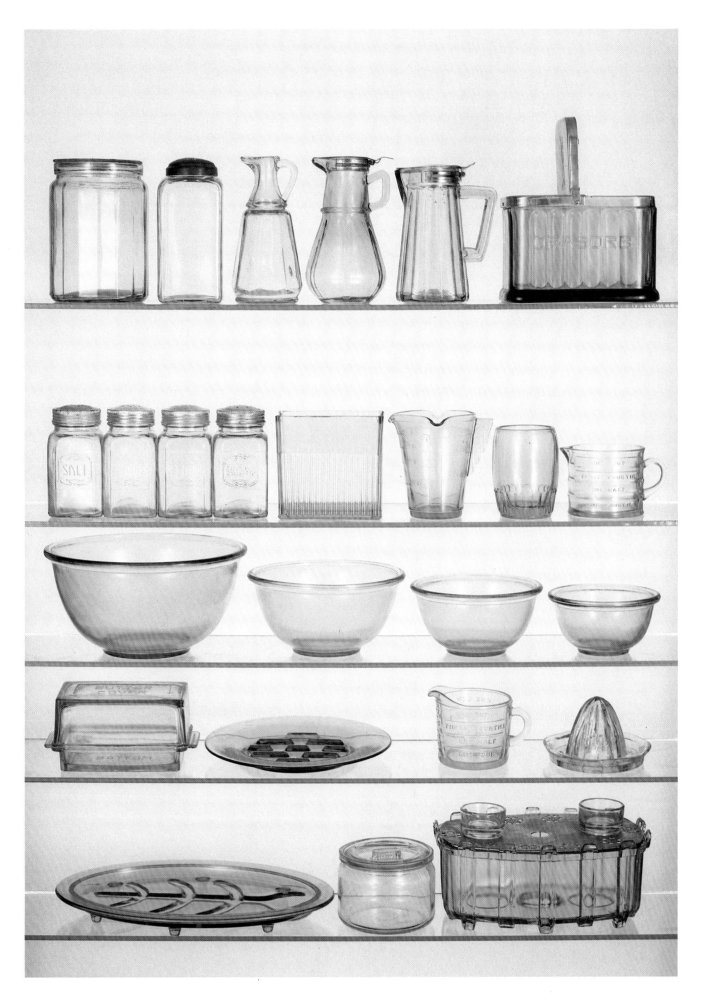

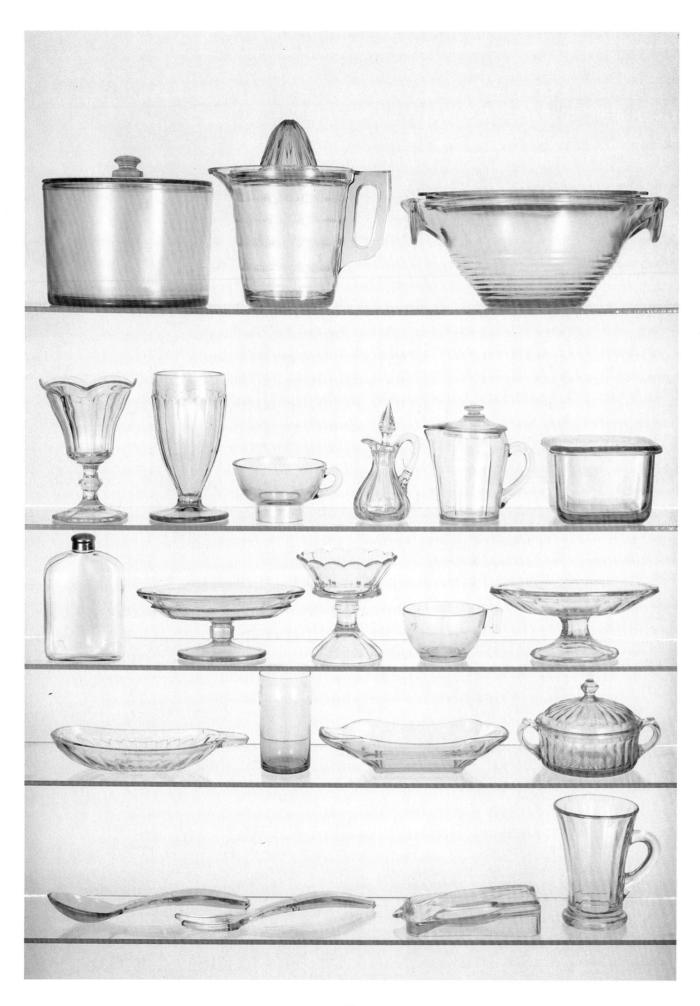

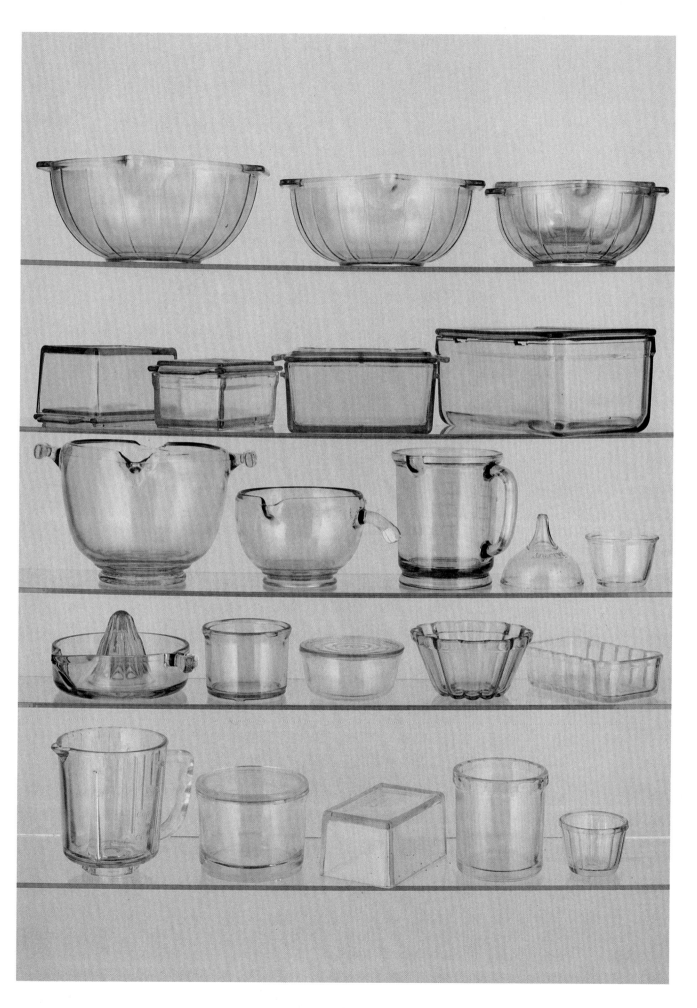

GREEN TRANSPARENT MISCELLANEOUS

The most desirable canister set for collectors of green to own is the Sneath set shown in Row 2 on page 51. Very few sets have been completed over the years. In Row 3, the "Zipper" set runs a close second, but it can be put together much easier and seems to have been a nationally distributed set.

Page 51

Row 1:	#1	Strawholder, tall	350.00–375.00
	#2	Strawholder, fancy base	350.00–400.00
	#3	Strawholder, short	300.00–350.00
	#4	Paden City, 'Rena' line tumbler	8.00– 10.00
	#5	Same, pitcher	35.00– 40.00
Row 2:	#1	Paden City syrup w/liner	40.00– 45.00
	#2	Bullet-shaped sugar shaker w/dots on top made by McKee	90.00–110.00
	#3-9	Sneath spice shakers, ea	30.00– 35.00
	#10	Sneath embossed TEA	125.00–150.00
	#11	Same, embossed COFFEE	175.00–200.00

Row 3:	#1	"Zipper" large canister	145.00–165.00
	#2	Same, embossed COFFEE	125.00–150.00
	#3	Same, embossed TEA	100.00–115.00
	#4-6	Same, spice shakers	30.00– 35.00
	#7	Holt soapsaver dish	20.00– 25.00
Row 4:	#1	Batter jug Paden City w/lid	65.00– 75.00
	#2	Paden City "Party Line" napkin holder	75.00– 85.00
	#3	Pitcher	35.00– 45.00
	#4	Jenkins pitcher	40.00– 45.00

Page 52

Row 1:	#1	Canister, sugar	85.00–100.00
	#2	Cocktail shaker	12.00– 15.00
	#3	Ring cocktail shaker	14.00– 16.00
	#4	Apothecary jar	25.00– 30.00
	#5	Cookie, frosted	40.00– 45.00
Row 2:	#1	Spouted mixing bowl	18.00– 20.00
	#2	Butter tub	25.00– 30.00
	#3-5	Three jar set	4.00– 50.00
	#6	Mustard	12.00– 15.00
	#7	Spouted bowl, 4½"	10.00– 12.50

Row 3:	#1	Canister, similar to first item in Row 1	25.00– 30.00
	#2	Punch ladle	25.00– 35.00
	#3	Cambridge fork	35.00– 40.00
	#4	Knife rest	12.00– 15.00
Row 4:	#1	Jenkins reamer pitcher w/lid shown beside it	500.00–550.00
	#3	Canister embossed TEA	35.00– 40.00
	#4	Salt	75.00– 85.00
	#5	Large salt	100.00–125.00

Page 53

Row 1:	#1	Churn	200.00–250.00
	#2	L.E. Smith cookie	60.00– 75.00
	#3	Imperial cocktail shaker	25.00– 30.00
	#4	Cocktail shaker (Sweet Ad-Aline painted on side)	20.00– 25.00
Row 2:	#1	Reamer, called "Speakeasy" by collectors	35.00– 40.00
	#2	Hocking pinched-in decanter	30.00– 35.00
	#3	Cookie jar	30.00– 35.00
	#4	Jar	30.00– 35.00
	#5	Paden City ftd. tumbler	8.00– 10.00

Row 2:	(Continued)		
	#6	Glass straw	3.00– 4.00
Row 3:	#1	Paden City sundae	22.50–25.00
	#2	Covered round dish, 7¼"	27.50–30.00
	#3	Same, 8¼"	32.50–35.00
	#4	Crock, 6¼"	37.50–40.00
Row 4:	#1	Tufglas refrigerator dish, 5⅞" sq.	20.00–25.00
	#2	Cold cream jar	8.00–10.00
	#3	Twisted towel bar	20.00–25.00
	#4	Coffee pot lid	5.00– 6.00
	#5	Drawer pull	5.00– 7.00

GREEN TRANSPARENT, Hocking Glass Company

Hocking green still can be found, but there are many new collectors so supply is drying up. The water bottle in Row 1, #3, page 55 is more abundant than previously thought. Price has now dropped. The round shakers (page 59, Row 4) command a higher price than most Hocking shakers.

Page 55

Row 1:	#1	Decanter, pinched in	35.00– 40.00
	#2	Water bottle	22.00– 25.00
	#3	Water bottle	35.00– 40.00
	#4	Water bottle	20.00– 22.00
	#5	Decanter (same stopper as Cameo)	35.00– 40.00
Row 2:	#1-6	Pretzel Set (6)	225.00–250.00
		Pitcher, 60 oz.	14.00– 16.00
		Pitcher, 80 oz.(not shown)	20.00– 25.00
		Mug, ea.	25.00– 28.00
		Pretzel jar	65.00– 75.00
Row 3:	#1, 2	Water bottles, 32 oz., 2 styles	18.00– 20.00
	#3	Same, 62 oz.	20.00– 22.00
	#4, 5	Water bottles, raised panels, 32 oz	16.00– 18.00
		Same, 62 oz.	18.00– 20.00

Page 56

Row 1:	#1-3	Paneled mixing bowl, 11½"	15.00–18.00
		10¼"	12.00–15.00
		9½"	10.00–12.00
Row 2:	#1, 3, 4	8½"	10.00–12.00
		7½"	7.00– 9.00
		6¾"	7.00– 9.00
	#2	8½" bowl, embossed Diamond Crystal Salt	15.00–18.00
Row 3:	#1-4	Mixing bowl, 9½"	10.00–12.00
		8¾"	8.00–10.00
		7¾"	8.00–10.00
		6¾"	6.00– 8.00
Row 4:	#1	Mixing bowl, 10½"	15.00–18.00
	#2	Batter bowl, handled	25.00–30.00
	#3	Batter bowl	25.00–28.00

Page 57

Row 1:	#1	Butter dish	20.00– 25.00
	#2	Block Optic butter dish	35.00– 40.00
	#3	Refrigerator dish, Block design, 4¼" x 4¾"	18.00– 20.00
Row 2:	#1-3	Panelled refrigerator dish, 8" x 8"	20.00– 25.00
		Same, 4" x 8"	12.00– 14.00
		Same, 4" x 4"	10.00– 12.00
Row 3:	#1	"Vegetable Freshener" embossed on top	85.00–100.00
	#2, 3	Indent handle, 4" x 4", refrigerator dish	12.00– 15.00
		Same, 4" x 8"	14.00– 16.00
Row 4:	#1-4	Oval refrigerator jars (2 style knobs), 8"	22.00– 25.00
		Same, 7"	20.00– 22.00
		Same, 6"	16.00– 18.00
Row 5:	#1	Crock, 8"	30.00– 40.00
		Crock, 6½" (not shown)	20.00– 25.00
	#2	Crock, 5"	18.00– 20.00
	#3, 4	Round refrigerator jar and cover, 9"	35.00– 40.00
		Same, 7" (not shown)	22.00– 25.00
		Same, 5"	18.00– 20.00

GREEN TRANSPARENT and FIRED-ON COLORS,
Hocking and Others

Hocking canisters remain the most popular of all those shown in this book, probably because they can be found. Those with perfect glass lids are difficult to find; the screw-type lid are easier to find, but less in demand. There is a 4-oz. provision jar to go with the other four in Row 3, page 59. I suspect that it is rare because it was never shown in Hocking's catalogues. Besides, what could you store in a 4-oz. provision jar?

Newly-made labels for Hocking or Owens-Illinois canisters can be ordered from: Lorrie Kitchen, 3905F Torrance, Toledo, OH 43612. Write for price and styles if your labels are missing.

There are beginning to be more collectors for the fired-on colors. You will find another photo of fired-on colors on page 71.

Page 59

Row 1: #1-5	Canisters, 47 oz. w/glass lid	37.50–40.00
#6-8	Shakers, ea.	10.00–12.00
Row 2: #1	Canister, screw-on lid, 64 oz.	35.00–40.00
#2, 3	Same, 40 oz.	35.00–37.50
#4	Same, 20 oz.	32.50–35.00
#5	Shaker, 8 oz., labeled "Domino Sugar"	12.00–15.00
#6, 7	Shakers, ea.	10.00–12.00
Row 3: #1-4	Provision jars, 64 oz.	30.00–35.00
	Same, 32 oz.	22.50–25.00
	Same, 16 oz.	14.00–16.00

Row 3: (Continued)		
	Same, 8 oz.	12.00–14.00
	Same, 4 oz. (not shown)	40.00–50.00
#5, 7	Round shakers, pr.	40.00–50.00
#6	Drip jar	25.00–30.00
Row 4: #1	Canister	25.00–30.00
#2-5	Smooth sided canister, 40 oz., screw-on lid	22.00–25.00
	Same, 20 oz.	18.00–20.00
	Same, 8 oz., ea.	9.00–11.00
#6, 7	Shakers, pr. (sold individually as sugar shakers)	25.00–35.00
#8, 9	Milk bottle caps, ea.	4.00– 5.00

Page 60

Row 1: #1	Cocktail shaker	18.00–20.00
#2	Cocktail shaker (pinched-in sides)	30.00–35.00
#3	Onion chopper	10.00–12.00
#4	Cigarette jar, ash tray on top	14.00–16.00
#5	Toothpick	8.00–10.00
#6	Electric beater	18.00–20.00
Row 2: #1	Measure cup	50.00–60.00
#2-4	Measure cups, ea.	22.00–25.00
#5	Syrup	20.00–22.50
#6	Cruet	15.00–18.00
#7	Ash tray	8.00–10.00

Row 3: #1	2-piece reamer	22.00–25.00
#2	Reamer pitcher	20.00–25.00
#3	2-piece reamer-ribbed pitcher	50.00–55.00
#4	2-piece reamer	20.00–22.50
Row 4: #1	Reamer, odd shade	12.50–15.00
#2	"Coke" bottle green	12.50–15.00
#3	Reamer, shade most collected	12.50–15.00
#4	Tab-handled reamer	10.00–12.00
#5	Tab-handled reamer	10.00–12.00

Page 61

Row 1: #1	Canister, glass lid, black	22.00–25.00
#2	Canister, Tulip design	12.00–15.00
#3	Canister (rabbits, ducks, lambs)	10.00–12.50
#4	Checkerboard sugar	18.00–20.00
#5	Same, flour	20.00–22.50
Row 2: #1-4	Shakers, black, ea.	6.00– 7.00
#5-7	Shakers, red, ea.	7.00– 8.00
#8	Shaker, green	4.00– 5.00
#9	Crisscross, 5¼" bowl	7.50– 8.50
Row 3: #1	Canister, screw-on lid, green	10.00–12.00

Row 3: (Continued)		
#2	Fire-King, 4⅞" bowl, green	2.00– 3.00
#3	Same, 6", red	3.50– 4.00
	Same 7¼" (not shown)	4.00– 4.50
#4	Same, 8⅜", blue	5.00– 6.00
Row 4: #1-4	Shakers, ea	3.50– 5.00
#5	Bowl, 10¼"	10.00–12.00
#6	Syrup, green rings	5.00– 7.50
#7	Marmalade, red ring w/spoon	7.00– 9.00

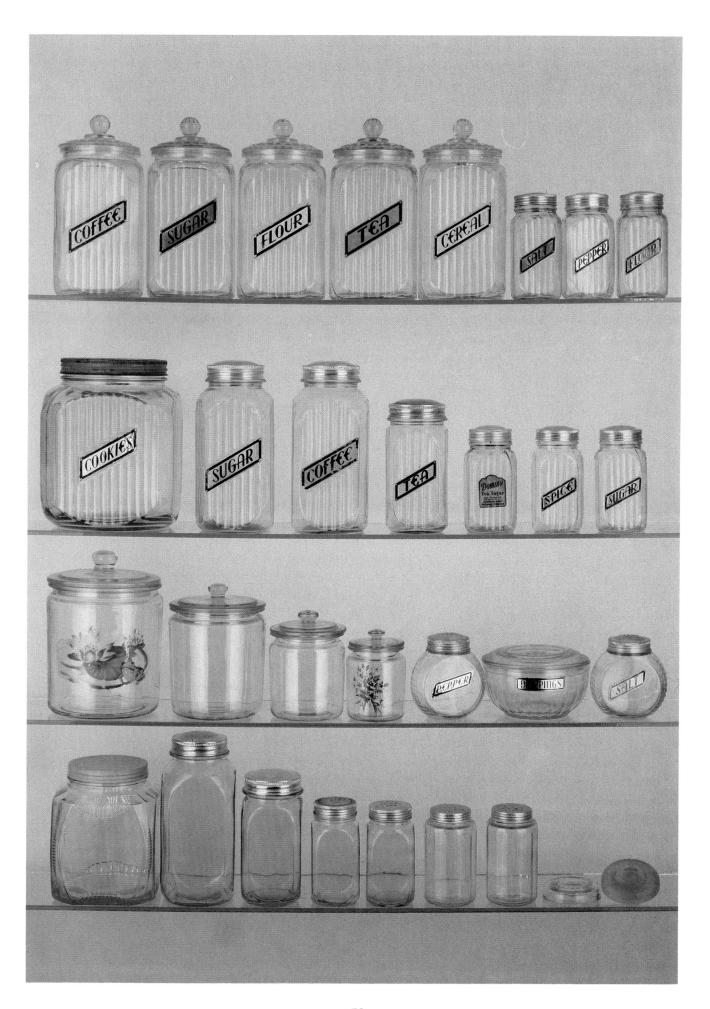

PINK

It turns out that the "so-called" sugar dispensers shown on page 63 Row 4, #5 and (shown complete on page 65 Row 2, #1) is a liquid dispenser for syrup or soap. I received several letters from the Chicago area with that information. Thank you! Next to that dispenser on page 65 is a Paramount napkin holder which can also be found in green and black. I would like find those for the next book if you have a spare.

That pair of embossed salt and pepper shakers on page 66 Row 5 have been reproduced in pink and cobalt blue; the latter color was never made originally. See Reproduction Section on page 221-223 for items with asterisk.

Row 1:	#1	Hex Optic stack set, Jeannette; base ($12.00-15.00);	
		lid ($8.00-10.00)	45.00– 55.00
	#2	Hex Optic flat-rim mixing bowl, 9"	20.00– 22.00
		Same, 10" (not shown)	22.00– 25.00
		Same, 8¼" (not shown)	16.00– 18.00
		Same, 7¼" (not shown)	12.00– 15.00
	#3	Hex Optic ruffled-edge mixing bowl, 8¼"	18.00– 20.00
		Same, 10½" (not shown)	22.00– 25.00
		Same, 6" (not shown)	15.00– 17.00
	#4	Ice bucket w/lid, Fry	150.00–175.00
Row 2:	#1	Butter box, 2 lb. embossed "B," Jeannette	90.00–110.00
	#2	Round salt	125.00–150.00
	#3, 4	Flat Jennyware shakers, pr.	45.00– 55.00
	#5	Tumbler	8.00– 10.00
	#6	Cruet	25.00– 30.00
	#7	Barber bottle	12.00– 15.00
Row 3:	#1, 2	Moisture proof shakers, pr.	110.00–125.00
	#3	Reamer, probably foreign	40.00– 45.00
		Same, sun-colored amethyst (not shown)	35.00– 45.00
		Same, crystal (not shown)	20.00– 25.00
	#4	Tumbler, imprinted Mission Juice	20.00– 25.00
	#5, 6	Quilted refrigerator jars, w/lid 8 oz.	15.00– 20.00
		4 oz.	12.00– 15.00
	#7	Stack sugar, creamer and lid	30.00– 32.00
	#8	Same only with place for salt and pepper	30.00– 35.00
		Set w/salt and pepper on above	50.00– 60.00
Row 4:	#1	MacBeth Evans stack set	40.00– 50.00
	#2	Ice bucket	20.00– 22.50
	#3	Ice bucket w/Sterling bear	40.00– 50.00
	#4	Reamer called "Tricia" by collectors	450.00–550.00
	#5	Dispenser w/insert (insert not shown)	85.00–100.00
Row 5:	#1	Reamer, unembossed "Orange Juice Extractor"	185.00–200.00
	#2	Paden City syrup jug	30.00– 35.00
	#3	New Martinsville syrup jug	35.00– 40.00
	#4, 5	Heisey Twist cruet, 2½ oz.	60.00– 70.00
		4 oz.	65.00– 75.00
	#6	Heisey Twist mustard w/spoon	60.00– 70.00
		w/o spoon	40.00– 50.00
	#7	Cambridge syrup	45.00– 55.00
Row 6:	#1	Bowl, 9¾" marked Cambridge	20.00– 22.00
	#2	Bowl, 7¾" plain bottom	8.00– 10.00
	#3	Bowl, 8", concentric rings in bottom	10.00– 12.00
	#4	Butter dish, bow-handled top	45.00– 50.00

PINK (Continued)

Page 65

Row 1: #1 Paden City "Party Line"
    crushed fruit/cookie jar 50.00– 60.00
  #2 Jenkins batter pitcher 100.00–115.00
  #3 Cambridge batter jug for
    waffle set 60.00– 70.00
  #4 Cocktail shaker 60.00– 65.00
Row 2: #1 Dispenser (possibly liquid
    soap or syrup) 85.00–100.00
  #2 Paramount napkin holder
    (U.S. Glass) 250.00–275.00
  #3 U.S. Glass "SHARI" cosmetic
    holder (2 pc.) 125.00–150.00
  #4 Stack set: sugar/creamer/
    plate/shakers 50.00– 60.00

Row 3: #1 Cambridge double gravy boat 20.00– 22.00
  #2 Imperial gravy boat 18.00– 20.00
  #3 Fenton "Ming" 2-piece reamer 400.00–500.00
  #4 Tufglas jello mold 22.00– 25.00
Row 4: #1 Paden City Party Line ice tub 22.00– 25.00
  #2 U.S. Glass 2-cup measure 125.00–150.00
  #3 Cambridge 1-cup measure 175.00–200.00
  #4 Stack sugar/creamer/lid 35.00– 40.00
  #5, 6 Curtain tie backs, ea. 8.00– 10.00
Row 5: #1, 2 Curtain tie backs, ea. 11.00– 14.00
  #3 Drawer pull, single 6.00– 7.00
  #4, 5 Single towel rods, 18", ea. 22.00– 25.00
  #6 Double towel rod 28.00– 30.00

Page 66

Hocking Glass Company

Row 1: #1 Pretzel jar 40.00–50.00
  #2-4 Canisters, plain, 40 oz. 35.00–40.00
    20 oz. (not shown) 30.00–35.00
    8 oz. 25.00–30.00
  #5 Refrigerator dish, 4" x 4",
    indented handles 10.00–12.50
  #6 Measure pitcher, 2 cup,
    ribbed 30.00–35.00

Federal Glass Company

Row 2: #1-4 Mixing bowl set (4) 35.00–45.00
    9½" 12.00–15.00
    8½" 10.00–12.00
    7½" 9.00–10.00
    6½" 7.00– 8.00
Row 3: #1, 2 &
    4 Refrigerator dish set (3) 45.00–60.00
    8" x 8" 30.00–32.00
    4" x 8" 18.00–20.00
    4" x 4" 6.00– 8.00
  #3 Refrigerator dish,
    3¾" x 5¼", w/legs 8.00–10.00
  #5 Butter dish, ¼ lb. 25.00–27.50
Row 4: #1 Butter dish, 1 lb. 35.00–40.00
  #2 4" x 4" vegetable embossed
    lid (asparagus) 18.00–20.00

Row 4: (Continued)
    4" x 8" vegetable embossed
    lid (not shown) 20.00– 25.00
  #3, 4 Round refrigerator dish, 4½" 12.00– 15.00
    Same, 5½" 10.00– 12.00
  #5 Reamer, Federal 85.00–100.00

Hazel Atlas Glass Company

Row 5: #1, 2 Mixing bowls, 11⅝"
    (not shown) 18.00– 20.00
    10⅝" (not shown) 15.00– 18.00
    9⅝" 10.00– 12.00
    8½" (not shown) 10.00– 12.00
    7⅝" 8.00– 10.00
    6⅝" (not shown) 6.00– 8.00
  #3, 4 Salt or pep, embossed *40.00– 45.00
  #5 Cruet 35.00– 40.00
  #6 Milk pitcher 15.00– 20.00
Row 6: #1-4 REST-WELL mixing bowl
    set (5) 45.00– 55.00
    9½" 15.00– 17.50
    8½" 10.00– 12.00
    7½" 8.00– 10.00
    6½" (not shown) 6.00– 8.00
    5½" 5.00– 6.00

Page 67

Row 1: #1 Utility pitcher 50.00–60.00
  #2 Slick-handle measure pitcher 40.00–45.00
  #3 Measure cup 45.00–50.00
  #4 Cruet 35.00–40.00
  #5 Cruet 25.00–30.00
  #6 Apothecary jar 20.00–22.00
Row 2: #1 Heisey cigarette and ash tray 55.00–65.00
  #2 Cruet set 65.00–75.00
  #3 Mixing bowl, 7" 12.00–14.00
    Same, 5" 8.00–10.00
    Same, 9" 15.00–18.00
  #4 Mug, "Adams Rib" 15.00–18.00
  #5 Ice pail 15.00–18.00
Row 3: #1 Round crock, 8", lid fits outside 35.00–40.00
  #2 Same, 6½" 25.00–30.00
  #3 Round refrigerator dish, tab
    handle 25.00–30.00

Row 3: (Continued)
  #4 "Kompakt" dish unit 40.00–50.00
Row 4: #1 Slick-handle mixing bowl,
    8¾" w/lid, spouted 35.00–40.00
    Same w/o lid 10.00–15.00
  #2 Slick-handle mixing bowl,
    9", (2 handles, spouted) 22.00–25.00
    Same w/lid 38.00–40.00
  #3 Slick handle bowl, 7½",
    spouted, "D&B" embossed 18.00–20.00
Row 5: #1 Slick handle 9" concentric
    ring bowl 20.00–22.00
    Same, w/lid 32.00–35.00
  #2 Snowflake cake plate 15.00–20.00
  #3 2-handle bowl, no spout, 9" 18.00–20.00

RED, TRANSPARENT and FIRED-ON COLORS

There are few red kitchens around, but red is a dramatic accent color; so there is a lot of demand for the red pieces shown here and on the next page. Fired-on colors really photograph nicely as you can see on page 71.

Page 69

Row 1:	#1	Boot cocktail shaker	150.00–175.00
	#2	Silex coffee pot	150.00–175.00
	#3	Decanter w/shot glass stopper	75.00– 85.00
Row 2:	#1	Cocktail shaker	30.00– 35.00
	#2	3 oz. tumbler that goes w/#1	3.00– 4.00
	#3	Barbell cocktail shaker (possibly New Martinsville)	75.00– 85.00

Row 2:	(Continued)		
	#4	Duncan Miller cocktail shaker	45.00– 50.00
	#5	Cocktail shaker	35.00– 40.00
Row 3:	#1	McKee batter pitcher	75.00– 85.00
	#2	Batter pitcher w/tray	125.00–150.00
	#3, 4	Tumble-up set	125.00–150.00

Page 70

Row 1:	#1	Hocking tumbler w/Old Reliable tea bags	10.00– 12.00
	#2, 3	Hocking water bottles, plain or ribbed	50.00– 65.00
	#4	Food chopper	20.00– 25.00
	#5	Strawholder (possibly 60's)	150.00–200.00
	#6	Hocking 24 oz. beater jar	40.00– 45.00
Row 2:	#1	Cambridge "Mt. Vernon" ice bucket	75.00– 85.00
	#2	Hocking ice bucket	30.00– 35.00
	#3	Cruet	90.00–100.00
	#4	Sugar shaker (maybe 60's)	100.00–125.00
	#5, 6	Wheaton Nuline shakers, pr.	40.00– 50.00
	#7, 8	Hocking shakers (possibly 60's), pr.	35.00– 45.00

Row 3:	#1	Imperial gravy & platter	150.00–175.00
	#2	Butter w/crystal top	95.00–105.00
	#3	Mixing bowl set (3)	165.00–185.00
		9¼"	90.00–100.00
		7¾"	45.00– 50.00
		6½"	30.00– 35.00
Row 4:	#1	Percolator top	12.00– 15.00
	#2	Knob escutcheon plate for door knob	10.00– 12.00
	#3	Double drawer pull	35.00– 45.00
	#4	Single drawer pull	20.00– 25.00
	#5, 6	Curtain rings, ea.	10.00– 12.00
	#7, 8	Feathered curtain tie backs, pr.	25.00– 35.00
Row 5:	#1	Trivet	40.00– 50.00
	#2	Tray (possibly for a New Martinsville set)	45.00– 50.00
	#3, 4	Fork & spoon set	125.00–150.00

Page 71

Row 1:	#1, 2	Rooster decanter w/4 shots	30.00–35.00
	#3	Sugar shaker (Gemco)	20.00–22.50
	#4	Canister, blue	15.00–18.00
	#5	Rooster canister, small	15.00–20.00
	#6	Same, medium	20.00–25.00
	#7	Same, large	30.00–35.00
Row 2:	#1	Measure, 2 cup	10.00–12.00
	#2	Pyrex, refrigerator jar, 3½" x 4¾"	4.00– 5.00
	#3	Hazel Atlas cup, green	32.00–35.00
	#4	Same, red	35.00–40.00
	#5, 6	Hocking ribbed shakers, blue, ea.	8.00–10.00
Row 3:	#1-3	Hocking, yellow, ea.	7.00– 9.00
	#4-6	Same, blue, ea.	10.00–12.00
	#7-10	Same, green, ea.	9.00–11.00

Row 4:	#1-5	Roman arch side panel, ea.	8.00–10.00
	#6	Glasbake, red cup	25.00–30.00
	#7, 8	Shakers, ea	4.00– 5.00
	#9	Reamer, tab handle, red	12.00–15.00
Row 5:	#1	Oval 7" jar, black	15.00–18.00
	#2, 3	Shaker (go with #1-3 in Row 4)	5.00– 6.00
	#4	Rolling pin, white	20.00–25.00
Row 6:	#1	Mustard (Gemco set)	4.00– 5.00
	#2	Salt bowl, same	8.00–10.00
	#3	Sugar shaker, same	12.00–15.00
	#4	Hazel Atlas sugar canister	25.00–30.00
	#5	Same, coffee	20.00–25.00
	#6	Same, tea	18.00–20.00
	#7	Hocking tea canister	12.50–15.00

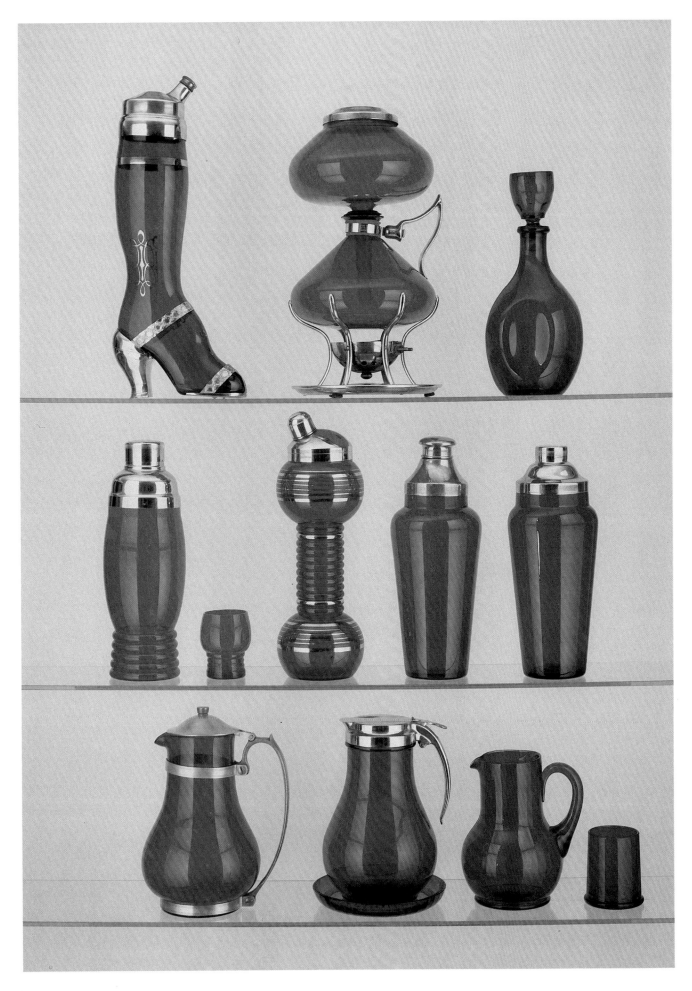

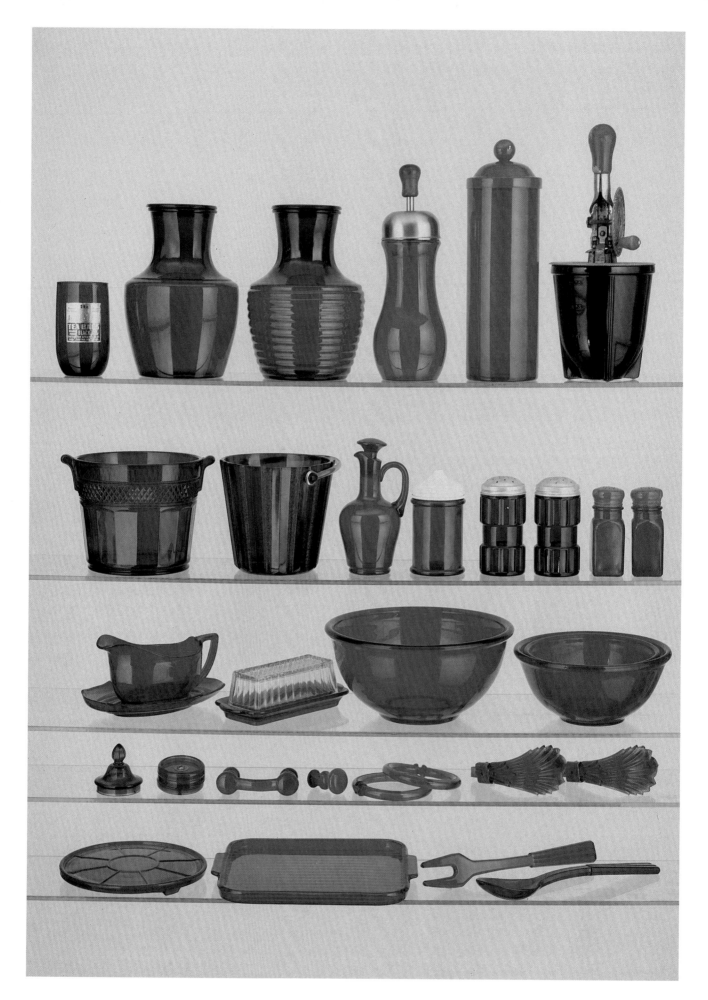

White

White is another kitchenware color that many collectors feel at home using as every day ware instead of the so called modern plastic and styrofoam. Most white is affordable and found without a lot of difficulty. The white grapefruit reamer in Row 3 on page 73 is unusual as is the fry reamer in Row 5 on page 75. Shakers need good lettering to command these prices!

Page 73   McKee Glass Company

Row 1: #1-4 Canister, 48 oz., ea   40.00– 45.00
       #5-8 Large shakers, ea   35.00– 40.00
Row 2: #1-4 Shakers, ea.   10.00– 12.00
       #5-8 Shakers, Roman arch side
           panel   10.00– 12.00
       #9 Canister, same design   40.00– 45.00
       #10 Dots 48 oz. canister   35.00– 40.00
Row 3: #1 Grapefruit reamer   250.00–350.00
       #2 Tea w/lid   25.00– 30.00
       #3 Bowl, 9" w/decal   20.00– 25.00

Row 3: (Continued)
       #4 2 cup measure w/decal   18.00– 20.00
Row 4: #1 Bowl, 9"   12.00– 15.00
       #2, 3 Shakers (good lettering!)   10.00– 12.00
       #4 Reamer, small   18.00– 20.00
       #5 Sunkist reamer   7.00– 10.00
Row 5: #1 Water dispenser   90.00–110.00
       #2 Glasbak measure cup   40.00– 45.00
       #3-5 Shakers, ea.   8.00– 10.00
       #6 Diamond Check shaker   12.50– 15.00

Page 74   Miscellaneous

Row 1: #1-4 Shakers, ea.   7.00– 9.00
       #5, 6 Shakers, marked
          "Electrochef"   6.00– 8.00
       #7 Shaker, "Home Soap
          Company" 12.00– 15.00
       #8 Spice set "Griffith's"   14.00–16.00
Row 2: #1, 2 Shakers, "Frank Tea &
          Spice Co." 10.00– 12.50
       #3 Napkin holder, "Fort Howard
          HANDI-NAP Napkins"   35.00–45.00
       #4 Same, "NAR-O-FOLD"   30.00–35.00
       #5 Refrigerator dish, "Breakstone's
          Fine Dairy Foods"   10.00–12.50

Row 2: (Continued)
       #6 "Androck" whipper   15.00– 17.50
Row 3: #1 U.S. Glass 2 cup reamer
          pitcher   125.00–150.00
       #2 Reamer, unembossed
          Fleur   50.00– 60.00
       #3 U.S. Glass tab handle   25.00– 30.00
       #4 Tab handle reamer   20.00– 25.00
Row 4: #1 Pickle ladle   12.00– 15.00
       #2 "Welch-ade" dispenser   125.00–150.00
       #3 Pitcher   20.00– 25.00
       #4 Embossed SALT, round   60.00– 75.00

Page 75   Hocking Glass Company Vitrock

Row 1: #1 Canister w/glass lid
          (rare)   75.00–85.00
       #2 Canister, 20 oz. screw-on
          lid   20.00–22.50
       #3 Shaker   6.00– 8.00
       #4-5 Mixing bowl, 6¾"   5.00– 6.00
          Same, 7½" (not shown)   6.00– 8.00
          Same, 8½" (not shown)   8.00–10.00
          Same, 9½" (not shown)   10.00–12.50
          Same, 10¼" (not shown)   12.50–15.00
          Same, 11¼"   15.00–18.00
Row 2: #1 "Blue Circle" flour   18.00–20.00
       #2-5 Same, shakers, ea.   7.50– 9.00
       #6, 7 "Black Circle" shakers, ea.   6.00– 7.50

Row 3: #1 Grease w/o label   18.00–20.00
          Same, w/label   20.00–25.00
       #2 4 cup measure w/lid   30.00–40.00
       #3 Reamer   18.00–20.00
       #4 Bowl, 10", red trim   15.00–20.00
Row 4: #1-3 "Red Circle" w/screw-on
          lids   30.00–33.00
       #4-6 Same, shakers, ea.   7.50– 9.00
Row 5: #1 "Red Circle w/flowers,"
          canister w/screw-on lid   30.00–33.00
       #2 Tab handle reamer   75.00–95.00
       #3 4" x 4" refrigerator dish   8.00–10.00
       #4 8" x 8" refrigerator dish   22.00–25.00

YELLOW, OPAQUE and TRANSPARENT, McKee, Hocking and Others

McKee's opaque yellow is called "Seville." Page 77 gives a representative example of this color which can be compared to Hocking's opaque yellow shown on page 78. Even though Hocking's yellow is more rare, there are fewer collectors; and that limits its price potential. Note the pinch decanter and the 4 cup measure in Row 1, #1 and #2. The #4 item in that row is a spoutless pitcher or a TEXAS mug. No one has ground off a spout; it was never there!

Page 77 McKee Glass Company

Row 1:	#1	Pinch decanter	75.00– 85.00
	#2	Measure, 4 cup, no handle	250.00–300.00
	#3	Measure,4 cup, ftd. w/handle	60.00– 70.00
	#4	4 cup dry measure (mug)	75.00– 95.00
Row 2:	#1	Bottoms down mug	125.00–135.00
	#2	Measure, 2 cup	25.00– 30.00
	#3-9	Salt or pepper, ea.	10.00– 12.00
		Flour or sugar, ea.	12.00– 14.00
Row 3:	#1	Grapefruit reamer	180.00–210.00
	#2	Sunkist reamer	35.00– 45.00
	#3	Refrigerator dish, 7¼" square	30.00– 35.00
Row 4:	#1	Butter dish	60.00– 65.00
	#2	4" x 5" refrigerator dish	12.00– 15.00
	#3	Measure cup, 2 spout	150.00–175.00
	#4	Bowl, 4¼"	10.00– 12.00
Row 5:	#1	Mixing bowl, 9¼"	20.00– 22.50
	#2	Same, 7½"	15.00– 18.00
	#3,4	Canister, 48 oz., ea.	50.00– 55.00

Page 78 Hocking Glass Company

Row 1:	#1-3	Canister, 40 oz., ea.	55.00–65.00
	#4,5	Canister, 20 oz., ea.	22.00–25.00
Row 2:	#1	Refrigerator jar, 4" x 4"	8.00–10.00
		Same, w/lid	15.00–18.00
	#2,3	Shaker, flour or sugar	10.00–12.00
	#4	Refrigerator dish, 6" x 6"	18.00–20.00
Row 3:	#1	Measure pitcher	175.00–200.00
	#2	Batter bowl	60.00– 75.00
Row 4:	#1	Refrigerator dish, 8" x 8"	40.00– 50.00
	#2, 4	Salt or pepper	10.00– 12.00
	#3	Grease jar	35.00– 40.00

Yellow Transparent
Page 79

Row 1:	#1	Fenton ice bucket	85.00– 100.00
	#2	U.S. Glass reamer pitcher	650.00–750.00
	#3	Glass for above set	15.00– 17.50
	#4	Fostoria ice bucket	30.00– 35.00
	#5	Fostoria oil and vinegar	65.00– 75.00
	#6	Fostoria "Mayfair" cruet	75.00– 85.00
Row 2:	#1	Fostoria oil and vinegar	45.00– 50.00
	#2	Fostoria "Mayfair" syrup & liner	55.00– 65.00
	#3	Sugar shaker	175.00–200.00
	#4	Hazel Atlas 2 cup reamer set	250.00–275.00
	#5	Hazel Atlas mug	30.00– 35.00
	#6	Duncan "Festive" gravy & ladle	30.00– 40.00
Row 3:	#1	Heisey syrup	65.00– 75.00
	#2	Heisey "Old Sandwich"	75.00– 85.00
	#3	Hazel Atlas 1 cup measure, 3 spout	175.00–225.00
Row 3:	(Continued)		
	#4	Hazel Atlas egg cup	3.00– 5.00
	#5	Canning funnel "C.W. Hart," Troy, N.Y.	35.00–45.00
	#6	Hazel Atlas refrigerator dish 4½" x 5"	30.00–35.00
Row 4:	#1	Hazel Atlas REST-WELL, mixing bowl, 8¾"	22.00–25.00
	#2	Same, 7¾"	20.00–22.00
	#3	Same, 6¾"	16.00–18.00
	#4	Same, 5¾"	12.00–15.00
Row 5:	#1	U.S. Glass slick handled batter bowl	30.00–35.00
	#2	Soap dish	18.00–20.00
	#3	Cambridge sugar cube tray	65.00–75.00
	#4	Spoon, salad size	30.00–35.00
	#5	Spoon, regular size	25.00–30.00

Part 2 Kitchen Items

BATTER JUGS and BATTER BOWLS

Batter jugs were made by many different companies in a multitude of colors. Most were made in sets consisting of a batter jug and lid, syrup and lid and underlying tray. Cobalt blue and red are the most sought colors, but Jadite (shown on the bottom row of page 81) is a prize also.

Page 83 shows a new category for this book. Although batter bowls came in many shapes and sizes, many of them did not survive. The "Turquoise Blue" at the bottom of the page took us four years to find. Cathy spotted it at Nashville, TN, last year.

The Hocking canister was a late arrival, and this was an all Hocking page. The top shows that "ARCO" Coffee was in the jar; but when empty, the jar was to become your cookies' home.

Page 81

Row 1:	#1	Paden City crystal w/black lids set	95.00–110.00
	#2	Paden City black set	175.00–200.00
	#3	Paden City pink w/black tray set	125.00–150.00
Row 2:	#1	Paden City syrup	30.00– 35.00
	#2	Paden City batter jug	40.00– 45.00
	#3	Paden City milk jug	35.00– 40.00
	#4	Paden City green batter jug	35.00– 40.00
	#5	Cambridge pink batter jug for waffle set	60.00– 70.00
	#6	Cambridge amber syrup jug	40.00– 50.00

Row 3:	#1	Jenkins #570 green batter jug	85.00–100.00
	#2	Green batter jug	75.00– 85.00
	#3	Square green batter jug	45.00– 55.00
	#4	Jenkins green batter jug	250.00–300.00
Row 4:	#1	Jenkins pink batter jug	100.00–115.00
	#2	Jeannette Jadite (bottom only- $50.00)	150.00–200.00
	#3	Liberty "American Pioneer" batter jug	150.00–165.00
	#4	Same, syrup jug	125.00–140.00

Page 82

Row 1:	#1	New Martinsville cobalt blue batter set	250.00–275.00
	#2	Same, amber	100.00–125.00
	#3	Red batter jug & liner	125.00–150.00
Row 2:	#1	New Martinsville green batter jug	50.00– 55.00
	#2	Same, syrup jug	40.00– 45.00
	#3	New Martinsville crystal batter w/green top	25.00– 30.00

Row 2:	(Continued)		
	#4	New Martinsville pink syrup jug	35.00–40.00
Row 3:	#1	McKee black batter	60.00–65.00
	#2	Same, white	55.00–60.00
	#3	Same, blue	70.00–80.00
	#4	Same, red	75.00–85.00

Page 83 All Anchor Hocking Glass Company

Row 1:	#1	Ribbed green	25.00– 30.00
	#2	Opaque yellow	60.00– 75.00
Row 2:	#1	Ribbed crystal	8.00– 10.00
	#2	Spiraled green	15.00– 18.00
	#3	"Mayfair" blue	100.00–125.00

Row 3:	#1	Cookie jar w/coffee lid	37.50–40.00
	#2	Fire-King (peach/grape)	12.00–15.00
Row 4:	#1	Same, Jadite	10.00–12.00
	#2	Same, "Turquoise Blue"	30.00–35.00

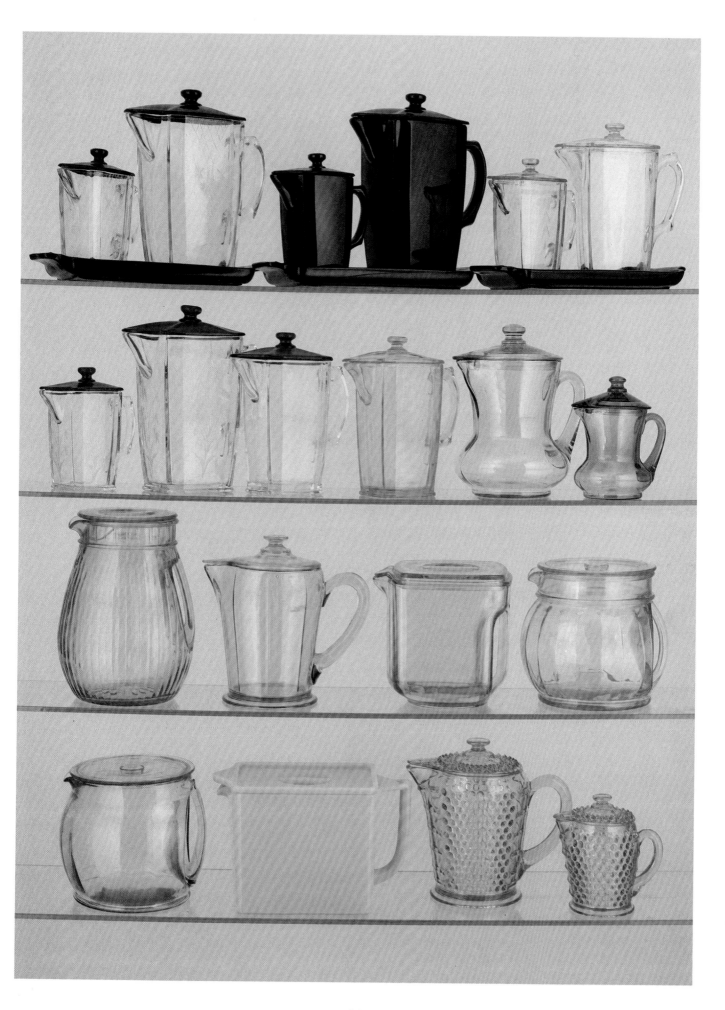

BUTTER DISHES, CHEESE DISHES and COFFEE POTS

Butter dishes can be found in several sizes from quarter pound up to two pounds. Evidently, many were premium items as indicated by the advertising found in and on them. In Row 2, #4 on page 85, the top says "Ask for 'Iowa creamery butter,' always good!" Other butters can be found in the **color** section of the book.

Page 85

Row 1:	#1	Custard, McKee	30.00– 35.00	*Row 4:*	(Continued)	
	#2	Skokie green, McKee	30.00– 35.00		#2 Jadite, dark,	35.00– 38.00
	#3	Seville yellow, McKee	60.00– 65.00		#3 Jadite, light,	30.00– 35.00
Row 2:	#1	Ships, McKee	20.00– 22.00		#4 Green,	32.50– 35.00
	#2	Red Dots	85.00–100.00		#5 Pink, (all pink)	50.00– 55.00
	#3	Delphite, McKee	155.00–170.00	*Row 5:*	#1 Ultra-marine, "Jennyware"	85.00– 90.00
	#4	Jadite bottom, metal			#2 Same, crystal	25.00– 30.00
		top ad	20.00–25.00		#3 Same, pink	65.00–70.00
Row 3:	#1,2	Amber ¼ lb., Federal,			#4 Pink, embossed Scotty	35.00– 40.00
		ea.	22.00– 25.00	*Row 6:*	#1 Green, embossed "B,"	
	#3	Crystal frosted, ¼ lb.			2 lb.	100.00–125.00
		Federal	12.00– 15.00		#2 Green, "Hex Optic"	60.00– 65.00
	#4	Amber 1 lb., Federal	25.00– 30.00		#3 Pink, embossed "B,"	
	#5	Amber tub, Federal	22.00– 25.00		2 lb.	90.00–110.00

Row 4: **Jeannette** tops embossed "BUTTER"

#1	Delphite,	145.00–155.00

Page 86

Row 1:	#1	Green, unknown	40.00– 45.00	*Row 4:*	#1, 3	"Crisscross," 1 lb., green	
	#2	Green, Hocking	20.00– 25.00			or pink	30.00– 35.00
	#3	Green, "Block Optic,"			#2	Same, crystal	15.00– 18.00
		Hocking	35.00– 40.00		#4	Same, cobalt blue	75.00– 85.00
Row 2:	#1, 3	Green, unknown	35.00– 40.00	*Row 5:*	#1, 3	Same, ¼ lb., green or	
	#2	Green "Clambroth,"				pink	30.00– 35.00
		Hocking	55.00– 65.00		#2	Same, crystal	10.00– 12.00
	#4	Refrigerator dish (sold as			#4	Same, cobalt blue	70.00– 80.00
		butter)	8.00– 10.00	*Row 6:*	#1	"Sanitary Refrigerator	
						Jar"	135.00–150.00

Row 3: **Hazel Atlas** tops embossed "BUTTER COVER"

#1	Green	35.00– 40.00		#2	Cheese, blue (foreign?)	90.00–115.00
#2	Crystal	18.00– 22.00		#3	"Hot & Cold" embossed	45.00– 50.00
#3	White	20.00– 25.00		#4	Cheese "Sanitary	
#4	Cobalt blue	150.00–165.00			Preserver"	30.00– 35.00

Page 87

Row 1:	#1	Silex, w/lid, large	90.00–100.00	*Row 2:*	(Continued)		
	#2	Silex, "2 cupper, drip			#2	Flashed red set: dripolator/	
		model"	20.00– 22.00			creamer/sugar/carafe	45.00–50.00
	#3	Red Silex, marked on		*Row 3:*	#1	Cory coffee maker	20.00–22.00
		bottom & band at			#2	McKee Glasbake	
		center	150.00–175.00			dripolator	50.00–60.00
	#4	Silex dripolator	35.00– 40.00		#3, 4	Glasbake ring decorated	
Row 2:	#1	Blue band dripolator				pots, ea.	25.00–30.00
		w/sugar creamer, set	35.00– 40.00				

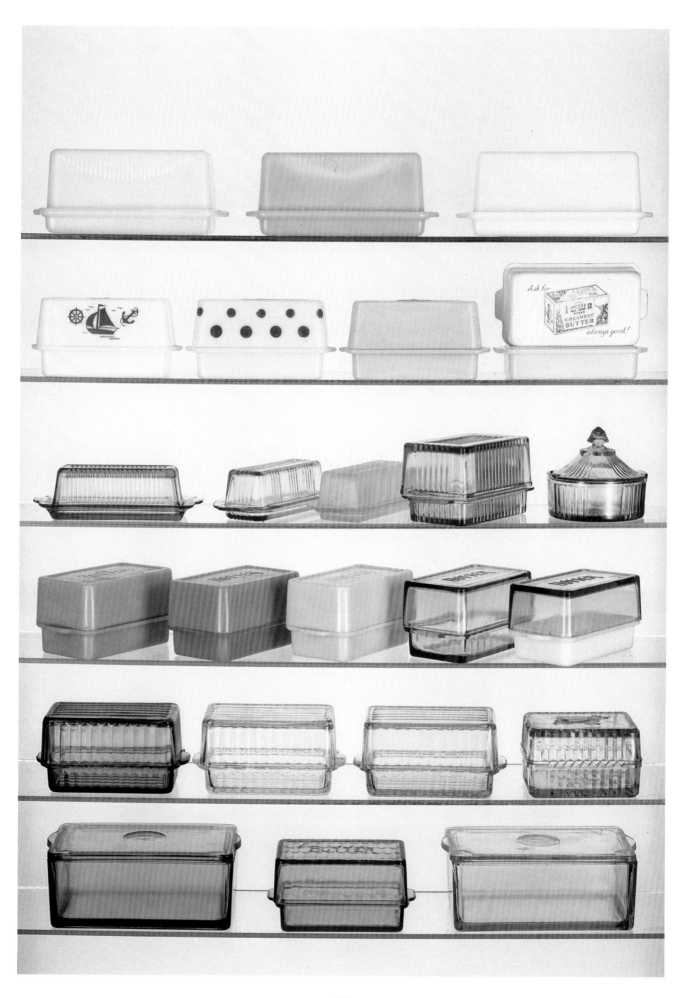

CRUETS and DISPENSERS (Refrigerator Type)

Page 89

Row 1: #1 Fostoria yellow "Trojan" 225.00–250.00
    #2 Fostoria blue "Fairfax,"
        w/stopper   100.00–125.00
    #3 Fostoria amber "Fairfax,"
        w/stopper   75.00– 85.00
    #4 Fostoria green "Mayfair" 75.00– 85.00
    #5 Same, yellow, w/stopper 75.00– 85.00
Row 2: #1 Fostoria "Colony"   30.00– 35.00
    #2 Fostoria yellow "Baroque,"
        w/stopper   200.00–225.00
    #3 Paden City pink #210
        line   40.00– 50.00
    #4 Same, green   40.00– 45.00
    #5 Jadite "Vinegar"   110.00–125.00
Row 3: #1 U.S. Glass (?) set on tray 65.00– 75.00
    #2 Imperial blue (not Heisey
        experimental blue) 65.00– 75.00
    #3 Same as #1, pink   65.00– 75.00

Row 3: (Continued)
    #4 Pink   35.00–40.00
Row 4: #1 U.S. Glass green   35.00–40.00
    #2 Same, crystal   12.00–15.00
    #3 Same, pink   25.00–30.00
    #4 Imperial, pink   25.00–30.00
    #5 New Martinsville "Janice"
        blue   40.00–50.00
    #6 New Martinsville "Radiance"
        crystal   15.00–20.00
Row 5: #1 Cambridge green   30.00–35.00
    #2 Same, amber   30.00–32.00
    #3 Cambridge, "Caprice"
        blue   50.00–55.00
    #4 Cambridge, "Apple Blos-
        som" pink   65.00–75.00
    #5 Cambridge, amber in
        Faberware   15.00–20.00

Page 90

Row 1: #1 Imperial "Canary Yellow"
        (vaseline)   45.00–50.00
    #2 Imperial green   30.00–35.00
    #3 Imperial "Cape Cod"   22.00–25.00
    #4 Imperial ribbed & beaded,
        pink   35.00–40.00
    #5 Same, no beads   30.00–35.00
    #6 Heisey, crystal   30.00–35.00
Row 2: #1 Lancaster Glass Company,
        yellow   65.00–75.00
    #2 Same, green   45.00–55.00
    #3 Pink blown (probably
        foreign)   60.00–70.00
    #4 Imperial pink   35.00–45.00
    #5 Fostoria "Garland"   50.00–60.00
    #6 Amber   30.00–35.00
Row 3: #1 Heisey "Old Sandwich"
        w/stopper   75.00–85.00
    #2 Heisey "Yeoman"   50.00–60.00
    #3 Heisey "Twist," 4 oz.,
        "Moongleam" green 75.00–85.00

Row 3: (Continued)
    #4 Same, "Flamingo" pink 65.00– 75.00
    #5 Same, 2½ oz.   60.00– 70.00
    #6 Imperial "Cape Cod" 15.00– 20.00
    #7 Duncan "Caribbean" blue 60.00– 65.00
Row 4: #1 Duncan "Canterbury" 15.00– 20.00
    #2 Red   90.00–100.00
    #3 Green   40.00– 50.00
    #4 Imperial's "Verde" green
        from Heisey "Crystolite"
        mold   15.00– 20.00
    #5 Hazel Atlas green   25.00– 30.00
    #6 Same, pink   35.00– 40.00
Row 5: #1, 2 U.S. Glass (?) dark
        green, ea.   32.00– 35.00
    #3 Pink   25.00– 30.00
    #4 Green   25.00– 30.00
    #5 Crystal   18.00– 20.00
    #6 Hocking green   15.00– 18.00

Page 91

Row 1: #1 L.E. Smith cobalt blue
        water dispenser   300.00–350.00
    #2 Same, light blue   150.00–175.00
    #3 McKee white dispenser 90.00–110.00
Row 2: #1 McKee Jade Green dis-
        penser, 5¼" tall   135.00–150.00
    #2 McKee Jade Green
        dispenser   75.00– 95.00

Row 2: (Continued)
    #3 McKee custard dispenser 110.00–125.00
Row 3: #1 McKee w/Jade Green
        top   120.00–135.00
    #2 Sneath Glass Co. green
        clambroth w/crystal top 45.00– 55.00
    #3 Water dispenser, Jade
        Green top   35.00– 45.00

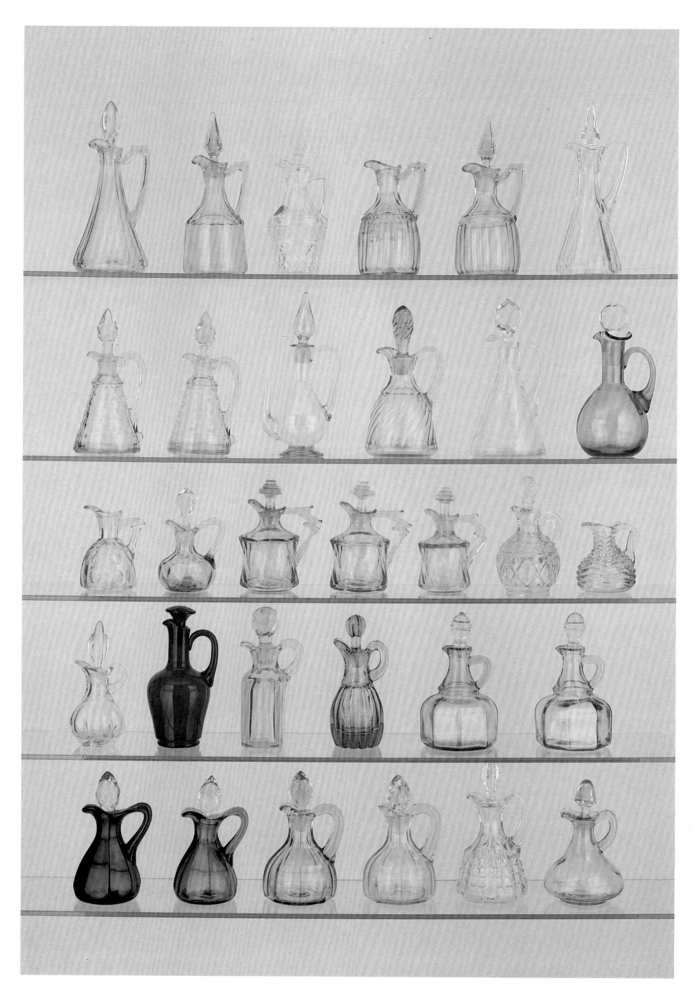

DISPENSERS, Drink and Juice

The popularity of these relics from restaurant and soda fountain days is overwhelming. Advertising shows seem to draw out the collectors with megabucks. There are usually four or five of these dispensers when a show begins, but rarely are there any left when it is over. One drawback, when it comes to displaying them, is size. Most are finding homes on antique bars. I suppose they remind folks of nickel drinks and dates with a beau where two straws shared the same soda.

Antique shows that feature old advertising items are among the best places to find kitchenware collectibles. In days past, that was where I bought many of my colored strawholders as well as other Kitchen related collectibles.

Page 93

Row 1:	#1	Crystal and Green (no name)	250.00–350.00
	#2	Samovar, green w/copper holder	175.00–250.00
Row 2:	#1	"Middleby" quality	175.00–200.00
	#2	"Orange Crush" type	200.00–250.00
	#3	Manufactured by E.B. Evans Co Philadelphia 33, Pa	225.00–250.00

Page 94

Row 1:	#1	Samovar yellow (possibly Paden City)	250.00–300.00
	#2	Mission Orange	175.00–200.00
	#3	Mission Grapefruit	250.00–300.00
Row 2:	#1	Paden City percolator, 3 piece, green	250.00–300.00
		Amber (not shown)	150.00–200.00
	#2	Mission Real Fruit Juice (pink)	125.00–150.00
	#3	Mission Real Fruit Juice (green)	150.00–175.00

Page 95

Row 1:	#1	Bireley's Orange Juice	300.00–350.00
	#2	Amber barrel and green base	225.00–250.00
	#3	Samovar green (possibly Paden City)	250.00–300.00
Row 2:	#1	Orange Crush	225.00–250.00

FUNNELS, GRAVY BOATS & ICE BUCKETS

While there are many collectors of ice buckets and gravy boats, I have never met a funnel collector per se. Pink and green funnels as well as some of the larger crystal funnels are not being collected as they once were. There is an abundance of crystal funnels since they were used in photography and gas stations as well as many pharmaceutical outlets.

Ice bucket collectors tell me that the Elegant ice buckets are easier to find of late, but they are more expensive! The buckets with polar bears have caught more than one collector's eye.

Page 97

Row 1:	#1	Funnel, 11", crystal	15.00– 20.00
	#2	Funnel, 9", crystal	10.00– 15.00
	#3	Funnel, 5", crystal	8.00– 10.00
	#4, 5	Funnel, 4" or 4½", crystal, ea.	4.00– 6.00
Row 2:	#1, 2	Funnel, 4½", ribbed or plain green	30.00– 35.00
	#3	Funnel, 4½", plain pink	30.00– 35.00
	#4	Funnel, yellow canning	35.00– 45.00
	#5	Funnel, Tufglas	75.00– 85.00
Row 3:	#1	Funnel, Radnt	50.00– 60.00
	#2	Cambridge green gravy & platter	45.00– 50.00

Row 3:	(Continued)		
	#3	Duncan "Festive" gravy & ladle	45.00– 50.00
Row 4:	#1	Imperial, red gravy & platter	150.00–175.00
	#2	Same, pink w/o platter	18.00– 20.00
	#3	Same, blue w/o platter	35.00– 40.00
Row 5:	#1	Cambridge, double gravy w/o platter	17.50– 20.00
	#2	Same, pink	20.00– 22.00
	#3	Same, blue	30.00– 35.00
	#4	Cambridge cream sauce boat for asparagus platter	20.00– 22.50

Ice Buckets
Page 98

Row 1:	#1	Jeannette "Hex Optic" w/reamer top, green	40.00–45.00
	#2	Van Deman "Black Forest", pink	50.00–60.00
	#3	Fostoria "Polar Bear"	30.00–35.00
	#4	McKee, green	20.00–25.00
Row 2:	#1	Fostoria "Swirl", blue	25.00–30.00
	#2	Fostoria "Colony"	50.00–60.00
	#3	Cambridge etched grapes	35.00–40.00
	#4	Fostoria, yellow	30.00–35.00
Row 3:	#1	Fostoria, pink	25.00–30.00
	#2	Fenton, jade	35.00–40.00
	#3	Same, black	40.00–50.00
	#4	Pink w/etched flower & square bottom	25.00–30.00

Row 4:	#1	Cambridge, "Decagon", amethyst	35.00–40.00
	#2	Same, amber	25.00–30.00
	#3	Cambridge, green	25.00–30.00
	#4	Cambridge, #731 or "Rosalie", blue	50.00–55.00
Row 5:	#1	Hocking "Frigidaire Ice Server"	10.00–12.50
	#2	Hocking, "Ring"	12.00–15.00
	#3	Paden City (?) pink	22.00–25.00
	#4	Crystal, Made in U.S.A. (English, other languages on side)	10.00–12.00

Page 99

Row 1:	#1	Fry w/lid, pink	150.00–175.00
	#2	Same, green	200.00–225.00
	#3	Fenton, w/lid, yellow	85.00–100.00
	#4	Fenton, w/lid, jade	75.00– 85.00
Row 2:	#1	Cambridge "Mt. Vernon", red	75.00– 85.00
	#2	Fenton, w/lid, green	55.00– 60.00
	#3	Fenton "Plymouth", red	50.00– 60.00
	#4	Green w/metal lid	20.00– 25.00
Row 3:	#1	Pink "Diamond"	25.00– 27.50
	#2	Green "Zig-Zag"	22.50– 25.00
	#3	Green	18.00– 20.00
	#4	Paden City "Party Line" w/etched flowers, pink	25.00– 30.00

Row 4:	#1	Paden City "Party Line", pink	25.00– 30.00
	#2	Same, amber	25.00– 27.50
	#3, 4	Paden City "Cupid", green or pink	85.00–100.00
Row 5:	#1	Paden City "Cupid" ice tub, pink	75.00– 85.00
	#2, 3	Paden City "Party Line" ice tub, ea.	22.00– 25.00
	#4	Green ice tub	16.00– 18.00

KNIVES and LADLES

There are some great knife collections in the country, and I would like to thank several collectors for volunteering to lend me knives to photograph. One California collector, Michelle Rosewitz, even brought her knives to be photographed at our four day session! Unfortunately, the only photographs that we were not able to use were those of the knives. Sometimes, even light meters lie to photographers!

Knife prices have now stabilized. Most of the "like" colors are selling in the same price range. All of the rarer knives are commanding higher prices!

Boxes add $3.00–5.00 to the price if nice. Boxes are placed near the knife found in that box. The box on the right in Row 1 of Page 101 says "New York World's Fair".

Page 103 ends the knives and starts out the ladle section.

Some knives are priced and not shown.

Page 101

		Pink (lt/dk)	Blue	Crystal	Green
Row 1:	#1-3 3 Star, 8½"	16.00– 19.00	17.00–20.00	8.00–10.00	
	#4-6 3 Star, 9¼"	16.00– 19.00	17.00–20.00	8.00–10.00	
Row 2:	#1, 2 3 Leaf Dur-X, 8½"	16.00– 19.00	17.00–20.00	8.00–10.00	17.00–19.00
	#3, 4 3 Leaf, Dur-X, 9¼"	18.00– 20.00		10.00–12.00	
	#5 Same, (light amber)	75.00–100.00			
	#6-8 5 Leaf, Dur-X, 8½"		17.00– 20.00	10.00–12.00	18.00-20.00

		Pink (lt/dk)	Amber	Crystal	Green
Row 3:	#1, 2 Rose spray, 8½"		100.00–125.00	40.00–50.00	
	#3 Plain handle, 8½"			12.00–15.00	25.00–30.00
	#4-6 Plain handle, 9¼"	25.00– 30.00			30.00–35.00
	#7 Same, (pinkish/amber)	40.00– 50.00			

Page 102

		Pink (lt/dk)	Amber	Crystal	Green
Row 1:	#1-3 Block, 8¼"	22.50– 27.50		12.00– 15.00	22.50–27.50
	#4-8 AER-FLO, 7½"	25.00– 30.00	100.00–125.00	15.00– 20.00	25.00–30.00
	#9 Same, (Forest Green)	90.00–100.00			
Row 2:	#1-3 Steel-ite	60.00– 70.00		25.00– 30.00	45.00–55.00
	#4 Stonex, 8¼", (white)	100.00–125.00			
	#5-8 Same, light or dark		90.00–110.00		35.00–50.00
Row 3:	#1 Candlewick, 8½"			125.00–150.00	
	#2 Dagger, 9¼"			55.00– 65.00	
	#3 Westmoreland, Thumb-guard, 9¼"			75.00– 85.00	
	#4 Same, Flowers			25.00– 30.00	
	#5 Same, minature (sample?)			125.00–150.00	
	#6-8 Buffalo Knife (B.K.Co.), 9¼"	30.00– 35.00		20.00– 22.00	30.00–35.00

Page 103 Knives top to bottom upper left picture.

	#1-3 Pinwheel and plain	8.00– 10.00
	#4-8 Colored handles/blades, ea.	20.00– 25.00
Upper Right:	**Ladles**	
	#1 White	25.00– 30.00
	#2 "Radiance", blue	75.00–100.00
	#3 White, Imperial	35.00– 40.00
Lower Left:		
	#1 Crystal	25.00– 30.00
	#2 Black	50.00– 60.00
	#3 Crystal	15.00– 25.00
	#4 Amber	25.00– 35.00
Lower Right:		
	#1 Duncan, "Caribbean"	30.00– 40.00
	#2 Same, "Hobnail"	25.00– 30.00
	#3, 4 Red handled	30.00– 40.00

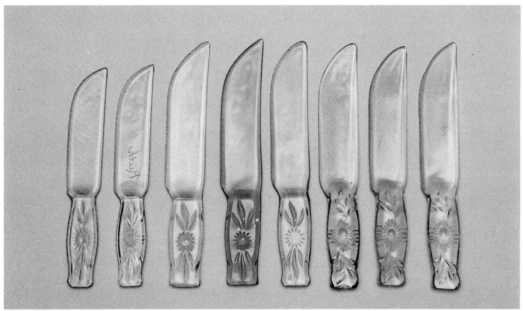

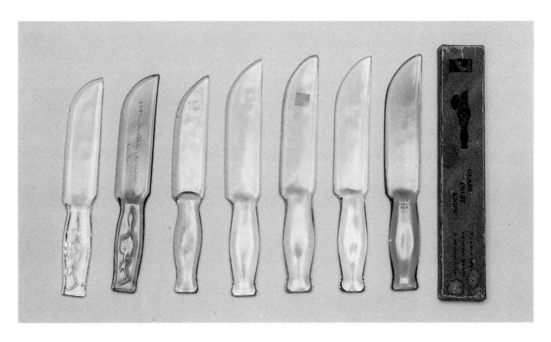

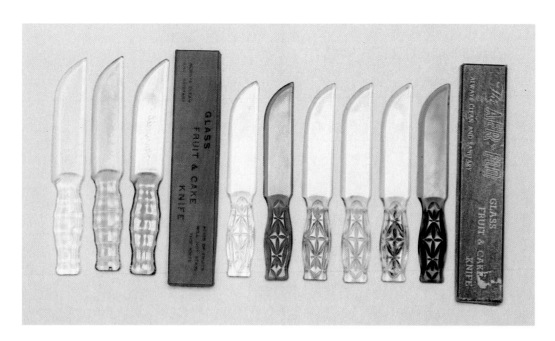

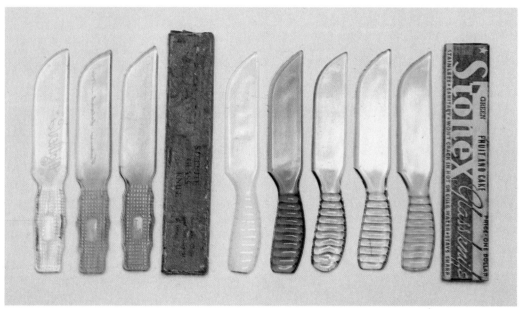

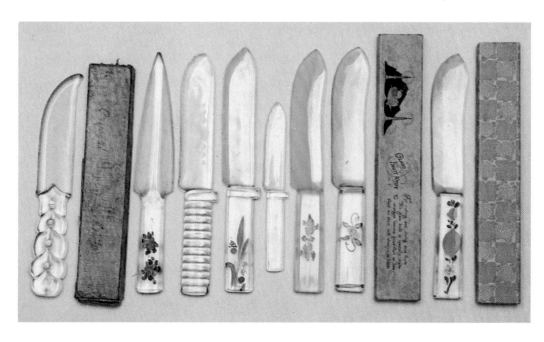

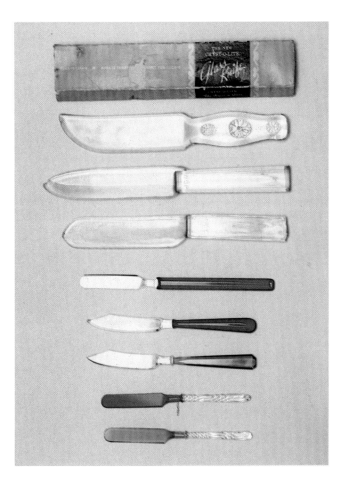

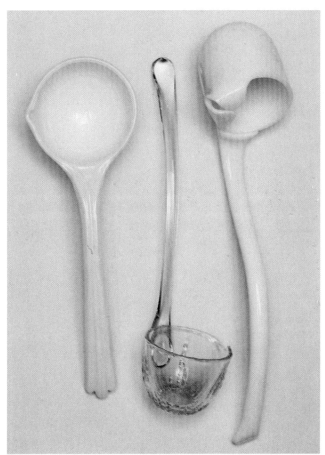

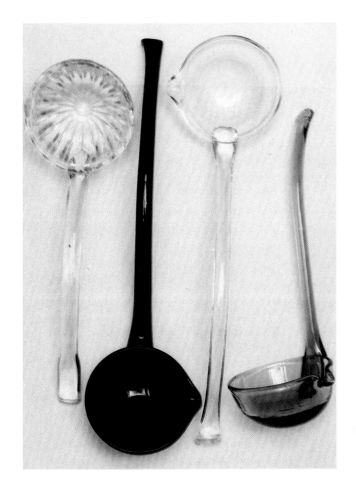

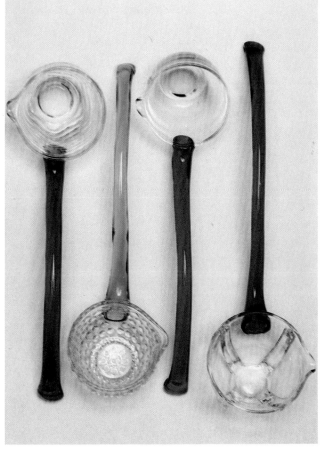

Ladles

Heisey and Fostoria ladles are those most in demand, although other company's ladles are collected. On the whole, colored Fostoria ladles have made the biggest price jump since the last book.

Page 105

Row 1: #1	Duncan, "Festive"	12.00–15.00
#2, 4	Pink	7.00– 9.00
#3, 5	Blue	12.00–15.00
Row 2: #1	Cambridge, pink	18.00–20.00
#2, 3	Same, green	14..00–16.00
#4	Same, Forest Green	20.00–22.00
#5	Same, Moonlight blue	30.00–35.00
#6	Same, amber	10.00–12.00

Column 1:

#1, 2	Green or yellow	10.00–12.00
#3	Blue, criss crossing design	12.00–14.00
#4, 5	Same, green or yellow	10.00–12.00

Column 2:

#1, 2	Fostoria, cobalt or light blue	30.00–35.00

Column 2: (Continued)

#3, 4	Same, amber, yellow or green	20.00–22.50
#5	Same, pink	22.00–25.00
#6	Same, crystal	8.00–10.00

Column 3:

#1	Cambridge, blue	20.00–22.00
#2-4	Same, green	8.00–10.00
#5	Same, crystal	5.00– 6.00

Column 4:

#1	Cambridge, amberina	30.00–33.00
#2	Same, Ivory	15.00–18.00
#3	Same, Primrose	20.00–25.00
#4, 5	Same, Azurite or Ebony	30.00–33.00

Page 106

Row 1: #1	Crystal, side spout	10.00–12.00
#2-4	Candlewick, ea.	5.00– 6.00
#5	Higbee, signed bee in bottom	20.00–25.00
Row 2: #1-4	Crystal, unusual shapes, ea.	5.00– 6.50

Column 1 & 2: **All ladles have rounded bottoms.**

#1 & 4-6	Crystal, plain & etched	3.00– 4.50
#2	Green	10.00–12.00
#3	Black	25.00–30.00
#7	Amethyst	20.00–22.00

Column 2:

#1, 2 & 4	"Clambroth" green or blue	18.00–20.00
#3, 7	Cobalt blue or black	25.00–30.00
#5, 6	Pink or amber	10.00–12.00

Column 3: **All ladles have wedge shaped handles.**

#1 & 10	White	6.00– 7.50
#2	Black	20.00–25.00
#3, 4 & 8	Blue, ea.	10.00–12.00
#5	Crystal	3.00– 4.00
#6, 7 & 9	Yellow, pink or green	8.00–10.00

Column 4: **All ladles have rounded handles.**

#1, 8	Forest green or light blue	10.00–12.00
#2, 5 & 10	Crystal, ea.	3.00– 4.00
#3, 4 & 6	Pink or green	8.00–10.00
#7	Amber	5.00– 6.00
#9	Black	20.00–25.00

Page 107

Row 1: #1-3	All iridized carnival colors	25.00–30.00
Row 2: #1,2	Heisey, Flamingo, ea.	20.00–22.50
#3,4	Same, Hawthorne	25.00–27.50
#5	Same, Moongleam	22.50–25.00

Column 1 & 2: **All ladles have flat bottoms.**

Column 1:

#1, 5	Flashed or amber	8.00–10.00
#2, 4, 6, 7	Yellow, green or pink	10.00–12.00
#3	Blue	15.00–18.00
#8	Cobalt blue, etched	28.00–32.00

Column 2:

#1	Cobalt blue	25.00–30.00
#2	Amethyst	20.00–22.00

Column 2: (Continued)

#3	Amber	5.00– 8.00
#4, 6	Frosted blue or vaseline	15.00–18.00
#5	Crystal	3.00– 4.00

Column 3: **All ladle knobs end in triangle shape.**

#1	Amber	5.00– 8.00
#2	Green	10.00–12.00
#3, 5	Amethyst or vaseline	20.00–25.00
#4	Red	30.00–35.00

Column 4: **All ladle knobs end in straight line.**

#1	Red	30.00–35.00
#2, 4	Frosted & vaseline	20.00–25.00
#3, 6	Flashed or amber	5.00– 8.00
#5	Green	10.00–12.00

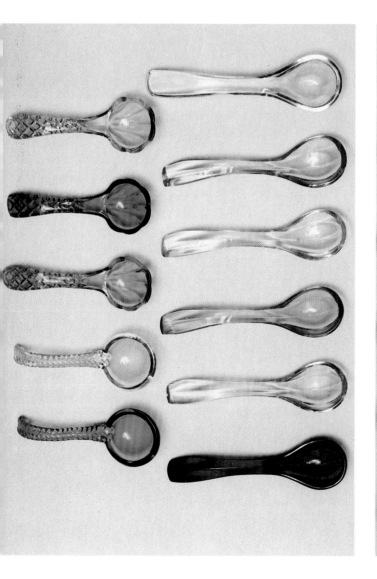

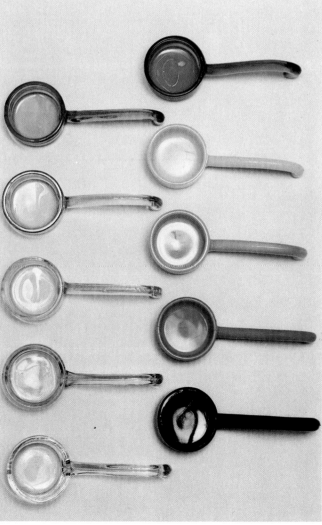

105

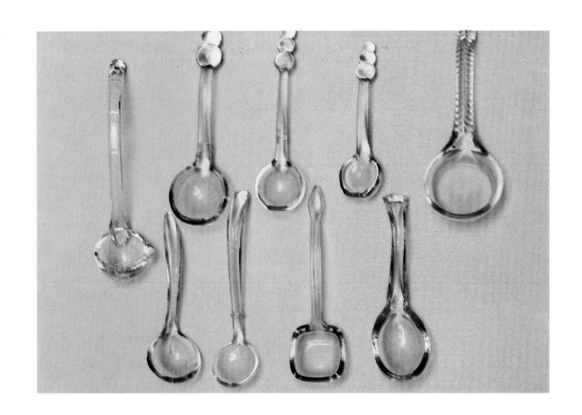

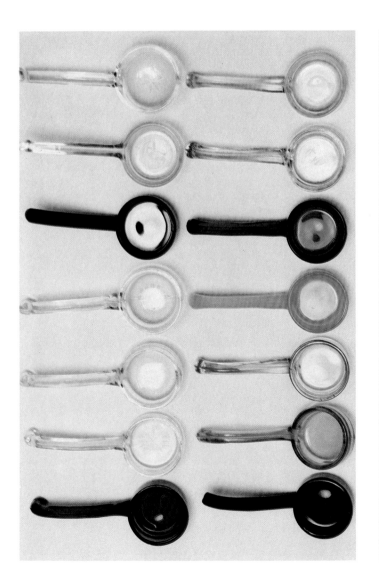

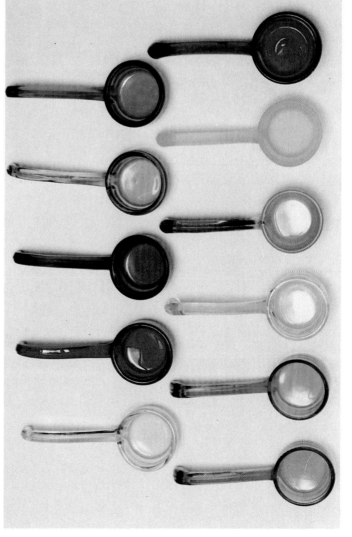

MEASURING CUPS — Advertising & Pattern Glass

Measuring cup prices vary greatly. Dealers who specialize in advertising items value these cups more highly than do measuring cup collectors. Many advertising dealers feel that any cup, including the later Fire King cups with ads, are worth at least $20.00. Most are, but not all! Only two people can decide the price — the buyer and the seller.

There are not many pattern glass measuring cups on the market, but those with lids are quite unusual. The lids are interchangeable on most of these cups.

Row 1: #1, 4, 5	Westmoreland w/measure lid (most have advertising in base such as "Finley Acker & Co.", highest grade at lowest cost		65.00–75.00
	w/o measure lid		35.00–40.00
#2, 3	Measurements below spout; w/o measure lid $60.00–65.00; w/lid		85.00–90.00
Row 2: #1-4	All Westmoreland w/ads, ea.		20.00–22.50
	"USE SILAS PIERCE PURE SPICE"		
	"USE SHEPARD'S DRAWING ROOM TEA"		
	"USE S.S.SLEEPER'S, Best of all Spices"		
	"USE GILLESPIE'S ORIENTAL FLOUR"		
#5	"ARCADE MFG. & CO., Freeport, Ill"		20.00–25.00
Row 3: #1	"SELLER'S," Pat. Dec. 8, 1925		25.00–30.00
#2	"J W POFF & SONS," Wrightsville, Pa.		20.00–22.50
#3	"NAPANEE" Dutch Kitchen Cabinet, world's finest kitchen cabinets, Coppes Bros. & Zook, Napanee, IN		20.00–30.00
#4	"PICKERINGS," Your credit is good, complete home furnishings, 10th & Penn, Pittsburgh		20.00–30.00
#5	"OWENS & CO."		20.00–30.00
Row 4: #1	"SILVERS," Brooklyn, Trademark (picture Brooklyn Bridge)		20.00–30.00
#2	"SAGINAW MILLING CO."		20.00–30.00
#3	"BUNKER HILL COFFEE"		20.00–30.00
#4	"CLOVERDALE" quality (4 leaf clover in red)		20.00–30.00
#5	"CAPITAL B BAND" Handy Cup Measure		25.00–30.00
Row 5: #1	"TIPPE CANOE," Kitchen Cabinets, none better		20.00–30.00
#2	"KEYSTONE FURN. CO.," The store that charges less, W King St., Lancaster, Pa.		20.00–25.00
#3	"HEALTH CLUB" Baking Powder for Success in every baking		20.00–30.00
#4	"STICKNEY & POOR" Boston Spice Co.		20.00–30.00
#5	"STICKNEY & POOR" Spice Co.		20.00–30.00
Row 6: #1	"SCOUT CABIN"		20.00–25.00
#2	"BROWN EKBERG" Golden Rule Store		20.00–30.00
#3	"ARMOUR", Use Armour's extract of beef		20.00–22.00
#4	"FLUFFO," "Be sure of success, use Fluffo shortening & salad oil"		20.00–22.00
#5	"CREAM DOVE" Brand Peanut Butter Salad Dressing, Cream Dove Mfg. in Binghamton, NY		20.00–30.00

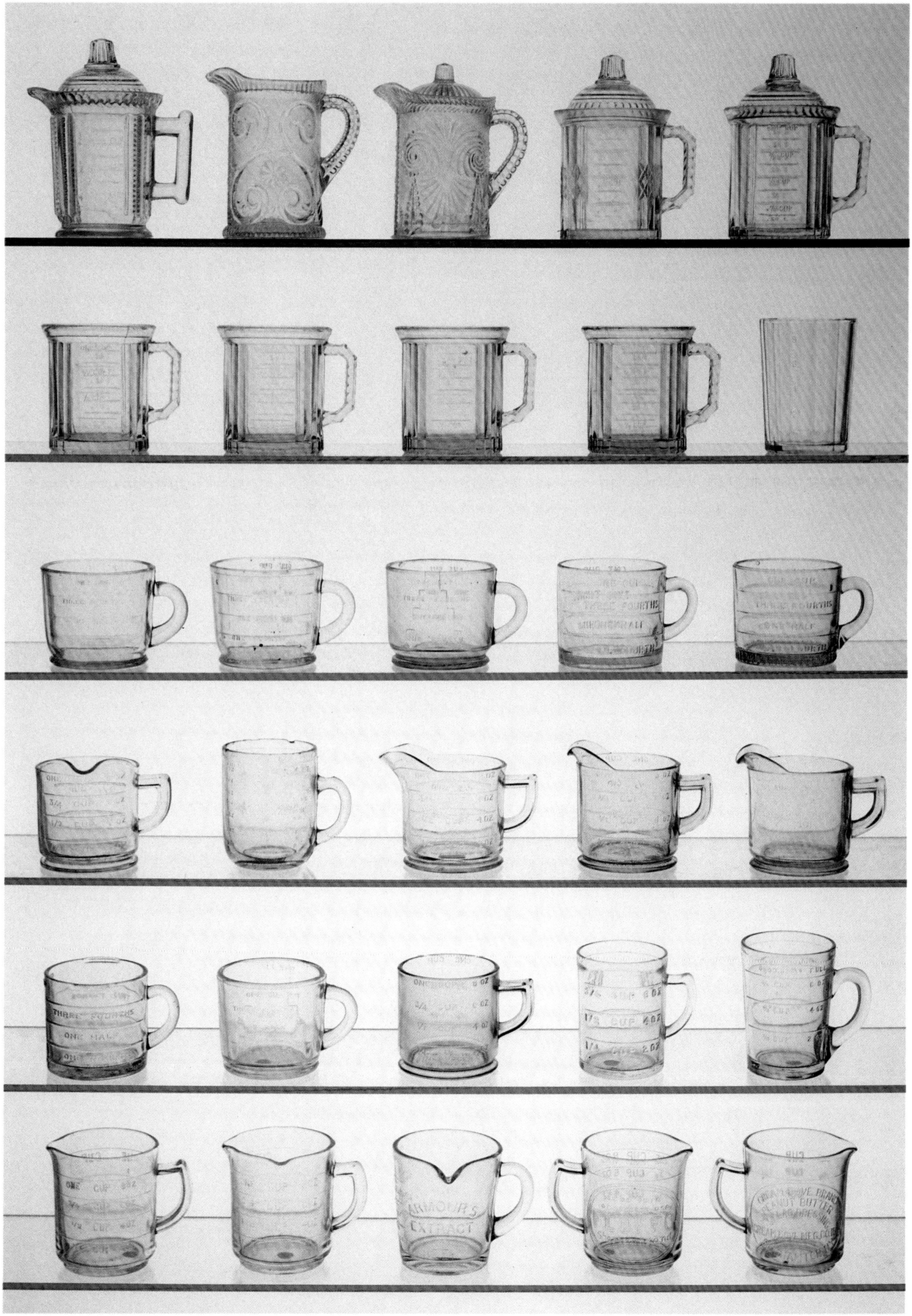
THREE FOURTHS
ARMOURS
EXTRACT

MEASURING CUPS

See Reproduction Section pages 221-223 for items with asterisk.

Page 111

Rows 1-3: **Jeannette Sets** except *Row 3:* Green $25.00–28.00; Pink $22.50–25.00

	Ultra-marine	Pink	Crystal	Delphite	Jadite
1 cup	35.00– 40.00	32.00– 35.00	25.00–30.00	40.00– 42.50	12.00–15.00
½ cup	32.00– 35.00	30.00– 35.00	22.00–25.00	32.00– 35.00	10.00–12.00
⅓ cup	25.00– 30.00	22.50– 27.50	17.50–20.00	25.00– 30.00	8.00–10.00
¼ cup	15.00– 20.00	15.00– 20.00	12.00–15.00	20.00– 25.00	5.00– 8.00
Set	110.00–125.00	100.00–120.00	80.00–90.00	110.00–125.00	35.00–45.00

Row 4:
#1	Mckee unembossed Glasbake, stippled bottom	10.00–12.00
#2	McKee Glasbake, fired-on red	25.00–30.00
#3	Glasbake, embossed	10.00–12.00
#4	Same, white	40.00–45.00
#5	Same, white w/red trim	45.00–50.00

Row 5:
#1, 2	Same, handle variations	10.00–12.00
#3	Radnt, 2 spout	50.00–55.00
#4	Glasbake (A.J. Novite & Sons; Charleston, 3 S.C.)	15.00–20.00

Row 6:

Chalaine Blue	Black	Seville Yellow	Jadite	Crystal	Caramel
500.00–550.00	500.00–550.00	150.00–175.00	125.00–145.00	50.00–55.00	400.00–500.00

Page 112

Row 1:
#1	Federal grn., w/o hdl., 3 spt.	18.00–20.00
#2	Same, crystal	10.00–12.00
#3	Same, amber	32.00–35.00
#4	Same, 3 spout, handle ad: "Easy Combomatic Washer/Dryer"	15.00–20.00
#5	Same, pink	50.00–55.00
#6	Same, amber	35.00–38.00

Row 2:
#1, 3	Same, solid hdl, 1 or 3 spt.	32.50–35.00
#2	Same, crystal	18.00–20.00
#4	Fry, 3 spout	55.00–65.00
#5	Same, 1 spout	40.00–50.00

Row 3:
#1-3	Hazel Atlas 3 spt white/trim	55.00–65.00
#4	Same, flashed green	32.00–35.00
#5, 6	Same, white or flashed red	35.00–40.00

Row 4:
#1, 2	Hazel Atlas 1 or 3 spout, green	15.00– 20.00
#3, 4	Same, pink, no embossing	30.00– 35.00
#5	Same, crystal	10.00– 12.00

Row 5:
#1	Hazel Atlas 3 spout, yellow	175.00–225.00
#2	Same, cobalt blue	*250.00–300.00
#3	Green, HA embosssed	15.00– 20.00
#4	Kellogg's embossed, pink	*17.00– 20.00
#5	Kellogg's embossed, green	*15.00– 17.50

Row 6:
#1	Cambridge, crystal	40.00– 50.00
#2	Heisey, crystal	175.00–200.00
#3, 4	Foreign, ea.	18.00– 20.00
#5	Blue foreign, EJKRONT (measures tea, coffee, wine)	35.00– 45.00
#6	Cobalt blue, foreign "SEPDELEN"	75.00– 85.00

Page 113

Row 1:
#1	Fire King, blue 3 spout	15.00– 18.00
#2	Fire King, blue 1 spout	12.00– 15.00
#3	Fire King, crystal w/red	3.00– 5.00
#4	Gr. emb "Urban's Liberty Flour"	40.00–50.00
#5	Pyrex, 2 spout	22.00– 25.00
#6	Same, 1 spout	8.00– 10.00

Row 2:
#1, 2	Green "Clambroth", ea.	135.00–150.00
#3-5	Hocking green, ea.	22.00– 25.00
#6	Hocking crystal	12.00– 15.00

Row 3:
#1	Gr. slick hdl., dry measure "Sellers"	40.00– 45.00
#2	Same, "E.E.Hamm", Hanover, Pa.	20.00– 22.00
#3, 5	U.S. Glass slick, hdl., 2 spout, ea.	25.00– 30.00
#4	Same, green, 1 spout	20.00– 25.00
#6	Crystal, dry measure	12.00– 15.00

Row 4:
#1	U.S. Glass pink, 1 spout	45.00– 50.00
#2, 3	U.S. Glass, green 1 or 3 spout	25.00– 30.00

Row 4: (Continued)
#4	Spoon measure	4.00– 5.00
#5	U.S. Glass, dry measure, white	175.00–200.00
#6	Paden City, green	95.00–100.00

Row 5:
#1	Green 3 spout	65.00– 75.00
#2	Crystal, oval	15.00– 20.00
#3	Same, green	40.00– 50.00
#4	Tufglas	85.00–100.00
#5, 6	Crystal, (rnd bot) or "Ideal" measure	25.00– 30.00

Row 6:
#1	Green, 1 spout	45.00– 55.00
#2, 4, 5	Crystal, 1 spt, or rectangular, ea.	12.00– 14.00
#3	Amber, 1 spout	150.00–175.00
#6	Amber	25.00– 30.00
#7, 8	Crystal "Root Tea"/"My Pet Milk"	20.00– 25.00

MEASURING CUPS (Rare and Unusual)

There are some hard to find measuring cups shown here. Several, including the Seville yellow and Chalaine blue four cup pitchers without handles, are the only ones ever found. The footed four cup pitchers in Delphite and "Caramel" are also unique at this writing! I reiterate from the last book that, "pricing unique pieces is at best, a guess."

It is difficult to attain an accurate price on items that have not been sold in years. For example, the Chalaine blue four cup without handles was bought for $100.00 in 1980. It has never been sold again! All I can use is an offer of $600.00 as a guide. The problem that occurs, if several turn up, is how many collectors are willing to pay $600.00 for the privilege of owning a Chalaine blue four cup measure.

Row 1:	#1	Chalaine Blue, 4 cup, no handle	500.00–600.00
	#2	Same, Seville yellow	250.00–300.00
	#3	Same, Jadite green	175.00–225.00
	#4	Same, crystal	30.00– 40.00
	#5	Tufglas, 4 cup	55.00– 65.00
Row 2:	#1	Seville yellow, 4 cup, ftd. w/hdl	60.00– 70.00
	#2	Same, Chalaine blue	150.00–175.00
	#3	Same, Jadite	25.00– 30.00
	#4	Same, Custard	25.00– 30.00
Row 3:	#1	Cambridge dry measure, green	175.00-200.00
	#2	Cambridge, 1 spout, 1 cup, pink	175.00-200.00
	#3	Same, green	175.00-200.00
	#4	U.S. Glass, 2 cup, pink	125.00–150.00
Row 4:	#1	McKee, 4 cup, Caramel	450.00–500.00
	#2	Same, Delphite	400.00–450.00
	#3	Unknown, green, 2 cups = 1 pt. & 20 oz. = 1 pt. on side	125.00–150.00

MEASURING CUP

IC778—8 oz., 3 in. high, heavy crystal, well finished, graduated for cups. 4 doz. in carton, 48 lbs..............Doz **48c**

GLASS MEASURING CUPS

No. 3   No. 2

No. 3—Half Pint Glass Measuring Cup. Packed 2 dozen to carton.
Per dozen $1.56
No. 2—Half Pint Glass Measuring Cup. acked 2 dozen to carton.
Per dozen $2.20

MEASURING CUPS

Emerald Green

1C2193 — 8 oz., 3 in. high, clear crystal, lipped, graduated forounces and pints. 2 doz. in carton, 30 lbs.....Doz **78c**

IC779—8 oz., 3¼ in. high, substantial pressed **emerald green** glass, graduated for ounces and cups. 2 doz. in carton, 25 lbs. **Doz 85c**

1C2183—2 styles, plain and side lip, 8 oz., 3¼ in. high, clear crystal, graduated for ounces and cups. Asstd. 3 doz. in carton. **Doz 79c**

MEASURING CUPS
CO-734 — 2 doz in carton, 18 lbs
Doz 78c
8 oz., 3⅝ in., pressed cup and ounce graduated.

MEASURING PITCHERS (2 Cups or More)

There are more measuring cup collectors than there are measuring pitcher collectors. Yet, there are some rarities in the pitchers. Most of the pitchers are bought by reamer collectors looking for bottoms to go with their reamer tops.

Owning decorated McKee two cup pitchers alone could fill several shelves in your china cabinet! Just take a look at the top three rows on Page 117. Considering that each of those designs could come on white or Custard as well as all the different colors gives an idea as to how many reamer tops you would need to complete these sets. **See Reproduction Section pages 221-223 for items marked with asterisk (*).**

Page 117

Rows 1-4 **All McKee 2 Cup**

Row 1:	#1, 2	"Diamond Check", red or black	22.00–25.00
	#3	Floral decal	18.00–20.00
	#4, 5	Green or red "Dots" on white	22.00–25.00
Row 2:	#1-3	Floral, black or red bows, ea.	22.00–25.00
	#4, 5	"Ships"	15.00–18.00
Row 3:	#1, 2	Black or orange "Dots" on custard	30.00–35.00
	#3	Custard w/red trim	18.00–20.00
	#4	Custard	15.00–18.00
	#5	Seville yellow	35.00–45.00
Row 4:	#1	Jadite	12.00–15.00
	#2	Delphite	55.00–75.00

Row 4:	(Continued)		
	#3	Fired-on green	10.00–12.00
	#4	Glasbake, crystal	18.00–20.00
Row 5:	#1, 2	U.S.Glass, slick handle, pink or green	35.00–40.00
	#3	Same, crystal	18.00–20.00
	#4	Iridized carnival	35.00–45.00
	#5	Crystal	8.00–10.00
Row 6:	**All Jeannette 2 Cup (Sunflower in bottom)**		
	#1	Green transparent	75.00–95.00
	#2	Jadite, dark	40.00–45.00
	#3	Jadite, light	12.00–15.00
	#4	Delphite	40.00–45.00

Page 118

Row 1:	#1	Hocking, 2 cup, green	15.00– 20.00
	#2	Same, ribbed, green	40.00– 45.00
	#3	Same, crystal	15.00– 20.00
	#4	Same, pink	30.00– 35.00
Row 2:	#1	Green "Clambroth"	85.00–100.00
	#2	Vitrock white w/lid	30.00– 40.00
	#3	Fire-King, 16 oz., 2 spout, blue	15.00– 18.00
		Same, crystal embossed "Diamond Crystal Shaker Salt"	20.00– 25.00
	#4	"Grandma's Old Time Measure", made in Italy, 1971	12.00– 15.00
Row 3:	#1	Embossed "A & J"	10.00– 12.00
	Hazel Atlas (Measuring & Mixing in base)		
	#2	Fired-on red	35.00– 40.00

Row 3:	(Continued)		
	#3, 4	White w/decorated colored bands	20.00– 25.00
Row 4:	#1, 3 & 4	White w/Dots	30.00– 35.00
	#2	Green w/white Dots	40.00– 45.00
	#5	Black floral decal	22.00– 25.00
Row 5:	#1	Iridized	85.00–100.00
	#2	Transparent green	15.00– 20.00
	#3	Crystal	8.00– 10.00
	#4	Crystal, "Spry"	12.50– 15.00
Row 6:	#1	Cobalt blue	*150.00–175.00
	#2	Pink, light	*40.00– 50.00
	#3	Pink, dark	*75.00– 90.00
	#4	Yellow	200.00–225.00

Page 119

Row 1:	#1	"Ocean Mills", Montreal, Canada (Man holding box of Chinese starch), 2½ pt.	60.00– 75.00
	#2	"Davis Baking Powder", ½ gal.	60.00– 75.00
	#3	½ gal.	40.00– 50.00
Row 2:	#1	1 qt.	25.00– 35.00
	#2	1 qt., green	250.00–300.00
	#3	Cambridge, 1 qt., measure top	75.00– 85.00
	#4	Baby formula, 20 oz., (foreign) Estans Materna	20.00– 25.00
Row 3:	#1	Umpire Glass Co., Pittsburgh, 1 qt.	20.00– 25.00

Row 3:	(Continued)		
	#2	Silvers Brooklyn Trademark, 1 qt.	20.00– 25.00
	#3	Sanitary Bess Mixer (embossed "4" inside a large "1")	175.00–200.00
	#4	Lighting Dasher Egg Beater Co., 1 pt.	18.00– 20.00
	#5	Hazel Atlas 4 cup crystal	12.00– 15.00
Row 4:	#1, 2	Hazel Atlas frosted green & white w/red trim, ea.	18.00– 20.00
	#3, 4	Hazel Atlas A&J green or white w/black trim, ea.	20.00– 25.00

MECHANICAL ATTACHMENTS

These accessory items make up some of the more unusual items in Kitchenware collecting. For those who collect colors, there are mechanical or hand beaters in almost every color. If you collect Fire King, there is a popcorn maker.

Besides the two ice cream makers known as sanitary freezers, there is a one quart maker shown at the bottom of page 122. An ice cube breaker is attached right beside it. I thought this was a great idea, but it was the first I had seen; so it may have not been too popular! This is quite heavy; we had to triple the glass shelves to hold the mixer and the ice cream maker.

Page 121

Row 1:	#1	"Keystone" beater, Pat. Dec. 1885, North Bros.	50.00– 60.00
	#2	Jewel "Beater Mixer" (mfg. by Juergens Bros., Minn., Mn.)	35.00– 40.00
	#3	Sanitary glass ice cream freezer (Consolidated Mfg. Co.)	60.00– 75.00
	#4	Mixer, 1 qt. capacity	8.00– 10.00
	#5	"Ladd" beater, green or pink (not shown)	30.00– 35.00
Row 2:	#1	Hydraulic "Niagara" food mixer (attaches to faucet)	25.00– 30.00
	#2	Thermos (mercury lined), "Higbee Hot/Cold Sanitary Bottle"	65.00– 75.00
	#3	Criss Cross food mixer (baby face on side)	25.00– 30.00
	#4	Mixer, bands at 4-8-12 oz. marks, Kamkap, Inc., U.S.A.	8.00– 10.00
	#5	Fire-King popcorn popper	35.00– 37.50
Row 3:	#1	"Vidrio" electric mixer w/cobalt blue base	85.00–100.00
	#2	Same, w/custard slag base	40.00– 45.00
	#3	"Chicago Electric" beater w/Jadite bottom	30.00– 35.00
	#4	"Challenge" w/Custard bottom	20.00– 25.00
	#5	"Kenmore" electric beater	20.00– 25.00

Page 122

Row 1:	#1	Delphite beater bowl	45.00– 55.00
	#2	Jadite beater bowl	25.00– 30.00
	#3	White beater bowl	12.50– 15.00
	#4	Iridized beater bowl	30.00– 35.00
	#5	Sanitary freezer	60.00– 75.00
Row 2:	#1	Handy Andy Juice Extractor	30.00– 35.00
	#2	Juice extractor	40.00– 50.00
	#3	Ser-Mor Juice Extractor Pat.	50.00– 60.00
	#4	Vidrio Products Corp. "Gem Squeezer" Cicero, Il.	40.00– 50.00
Row 3:	#1	Mixer, w/Chalaine bowl	75.00–100.00
	#2	"Deluxe Lightning One Quart Ice Cream Maker" w/Lightning Ice Cube Breaker by North Brothers	65.00–100.00

Page 123

Row 1:	#1	"J. Hutchanson" Trademark S&S Long Island (Mayonnaise)	100.00–125.00
	#2	Cobalt beater	75.00–100.00
	#3	Ultra-marine beater	50.00– 55.00
	#4	Pink beater	30.00– 35.00
Row 2:	#1	"Bromo-Seltzer" dispenser	115.00–135.00
	#2	"Ladd" mixer churn #2	75.00– 85.00
	#3	Mixer (similar to Keystone)	50.00– 60.00
	#4	"Silver & Co." food mixer	20.00– 25.00
	#5	"Bordens" Pat. Mar. 30, 1915	18.00– 22.00

MUGS

There are beginning to be more mug collectors than in the past. Many of these collectors are not aware that Kitchenware collectors also seek mugs to go along with their glassware.

The "Bottoms Down" mugs on Row 4 always create the most interesting comments from non collectors. At mall Antique shows, the little old ladies always look embarrassed about picking one up. Not much later, guess who comes back to show a friend?

The most expensive is the pink Colonial shown in Row 3. This also comes in green, but only three have ever been found in that color!

The last mug on the bottom Row is Moondrops. This mug can be found in several colors as well as two sizes.

Note the ad below for a "Beer Set" featuring the mug shown in Row 3: #3. These sets were made by Hocking and today, would fetch $225.00-250.00 as shown.

Row 1: #1	Green root beer	25.00– 30.00
#2	Same pink	22.00– 25.00
#3	Pink frosted root beer	25.00– 30.00
#4	Yellow root beer	30.00– 35.00
#5	Amber	35.00– 38.00
Row 2: #1	Forest Green, Cambridge	40.00– 45.00
#2	Yellow, same	35.00– 40.00
#3	Crystal, Heisey "Old Sand-wich" pilsner	20.00– 30.00
#4	Pink, called "Adam's Rib" by collectors	15.00– 18.00
#4	Same, green	20.00– 25.00
Row 3: #1	Colonial, pink, Hocking	350.00–375.00
#2	Black, "Genolite"	30.00– 35.00
#3	Green, pretzel, Hocking	25.00– 28.00
#4	Peacock blue	25.00– 30.00
#5	Forest Green, Cambridge "Mt. Vernon"	30.00– 35.00
Row 4: #1	Green soda fountain type	20.00– 25.00
#2	Same, apple green	20.00– 25.00

Row 4: (Continued)		
#3	Seville yellow, McKee "Bottoms Down"	125.00–135.00
#4	Same, Jadite	125.00–135.00
#5	Green, Imperial "Chesterfield"	22.00– 25.00
#6	Same, amber	20.00– 22.50
Row 5: #1	Red, New Martinsville	22.50– 25.00
#2	Light amethyst	17.50– 20.00
#3	Red, Cambridge "Tally-Ho"	22.50– 25.00
#4	Green, Hobnail	17.50– 20.00
#5	Green	15.00– 17.50
#6	Amber, applied handle	22.50– 25.00
Row 6: #1	Pink, footed Jeannette	20.00– 22.00
#2	Same, green	22.50– 25.00
#3	Green, Fostoria "Priscilla"	12.50– 15.00
#4	Green	35.00– 40.00
#5	Cobalt, New Martinsville "Moondrops"	25.00– 30.00

8-PC. BEER SETS
GREEN GLASS . . . OPTIC PATTERN

80 oz. jug, six 12 oz. handled mugs, 10 in. covered pretzel or cookie jar, pressed green glass.
50R-2075—1 set in carton, 12 lbs......Set **.95**

NAPKIN HOLDERS

Napkin Holders are turning out to be one of the most difficult items to photograph. They are all approximately the same size and shape. Since they are flat, details are hidden. That does not take into consideration the white or black ones. The whites disappear from the photo if you light from the back. The blacks vanish if you light from the front. Just one of the minor details that we encounter as we go along in a four day picture taking marathon.

The "Paramount" napkin holder shown below was found a couple of weeks after we finished the large photo. This "Paramount" also comes in green and black. I could use either color next time if you have one for sale. All colors are selling in the $250.00–275.00 range.

The light blue in Row 2: #3 may be a letter holder; but in any case, it is of foreign manufacture.

Row 1:	#1	White, NAR-O-FOLD, "Property of trade Nar-O-Fold mark Napkin Company, Chicago, reg. U.S.A.	30.00– 35.00
	#2	Frosted crystal	30.00– 35.00
	#3	Crystal, vertical ribbed	30.00– 35.00
	#4	Black, same as #1	115.00–135.00
Row 2:	#1	Crystal, horizontal ribs, L.E. Smith	32.50– 37.50
	#2	Forest Green	75.00– 85.00
	#3	Light blue, foreign	50.00– 65.00
	#4	White, Paden City "Party Line"	35.00– 45.00
Row 3:	#1	Pink, Paden City "Party Line"	95.00–110.00
	#2	Same, green	70.00– 80.00
	#3	Same, black	115.00–125.00

Row 3:	(Continued)		
	#4	Same, crystal	35.00– 45.00
Row 4:	#1	Green "Clambroth", SERV-ALL	100.00–135.00
	#2	Same, opal white	45.00– 55.00
	#3	Same, white	45.00– 55.00
	#4	White, Ft. Howard HANDI-NAP	35.00– 45.00
	#5	White, SLEN-DR-FOLD	40.00– 50.00
Row 5:	#1	White, FAN FOLD, Property of Diana Mfg., Green Bay	60.00– 65.00
	#2	Green, FAN FOLD, no other embossing	85.00– 95.00
	#3	Same, Forest green	95.00–110.00
	#4	Green, same as #1	85.00– 95.00
	#5	Crystal, same as #2	45.00– 55.00

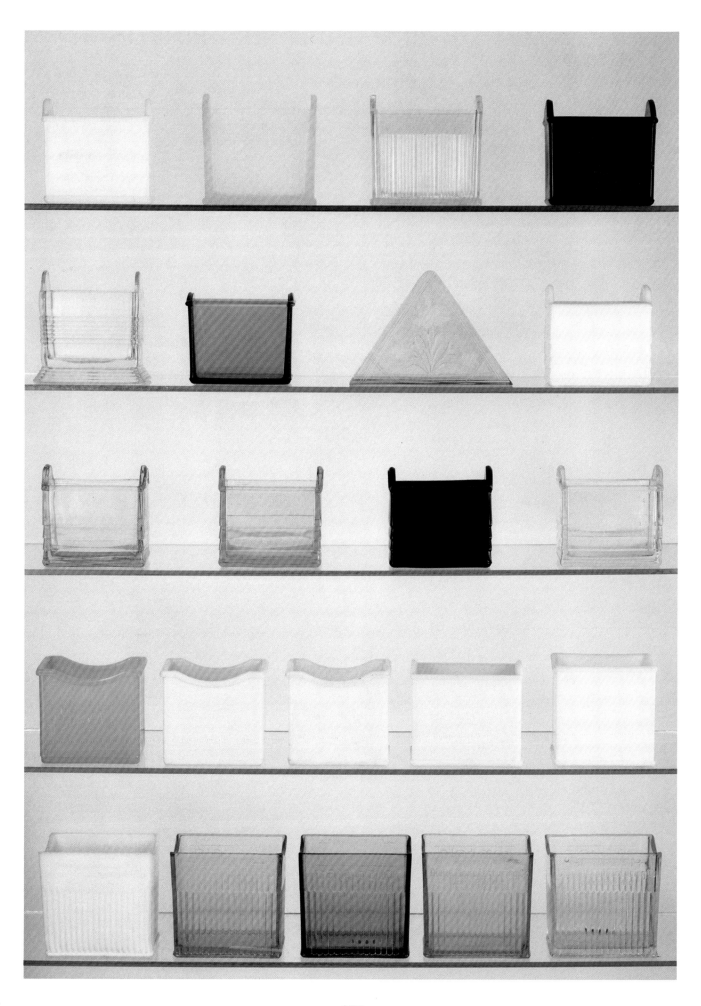

OIL & VINEGAR or FRENCH DRESSING BOTTLES

Demand for these items has increased since the last book. Collectors are looking for the better known etched patterns in Fostoria and Cambridge. While plain or unetched varieties sell, it is not as fast or at as high a price. Amber colored bottles are the slowest to sell no matter which company made them.

The correct stopper for the pyramid shaped bottle can be seen on page 43. Over the years many bottles had substitute stoppers added. Like lids and cups, many a stopper dropped! Note that often colored bottles have crystal stoppers.

Row 1:	#1	Paden City, green	37.50– 42.50
	#2	Same, pink	45.00– 50.00
	#3	Cambridge, etched pattern, green	65.00– 75.00
	#4	Same, no etching	30.00– 35.00
	#5	Cambridge, amber w/crystal stopper	25.00– 30.00
	#6	Same, w/amber stopper	35.00– 40.00
	#7	McKee set (late 1940's)	20.00– 25.00
Row 2:	#1	Cambridge "Rosalie" (#731), pink	85.00–100.00
	#2	Same, green	90.00–110.00
	#3, 5, 7	Cambridge crystal, ea.	15.00– 18.00
	#4	Cambridge w/sterling stopper	30.00– 35.00
	#6	Hawkes, green	60.00– 65.00
Row 3:	#1	Heisey, "Flamingo" pink	50.00– 65.00
	#2	Same, crystal ("Mfg. under license granted by T.G. Hawkes & Co.; Fill w/vinegar to line marked Vinegar, w/oil to line marked Oil, salt & pepper, etc., to taste, shake & you have perfect dressing")	30.00– 35.00
	#3	Heisey "Twist", pink	65.00– 75.00
	#4, 9	Fostoria amber, ea.	30.00– 35.00
	#5	Fostoria w/sterling top	20.00– 22.00
	#6, 7	Fostoria, yellow or green	65.00– 75.00
	#8	Fostoria yellow w/crystal top	45.00– 50.00
Row 4:	#1	Paden City "Party Line", pink	55.00– 65.00
	#2	Unknown "pyramid" style (wrong stopper; see p.43)	45.00– 55.00
	#3	Cambridge set, 3 pc. pink	45.00– 50.00
	#4	Crackle set (possibly Cambridge)	35.00– 40.00
	#5	Yellow	22.50– 25.00
	#6	Cambridge pink	15.00– 20.00
	#7	Amber	22.00– 25.00

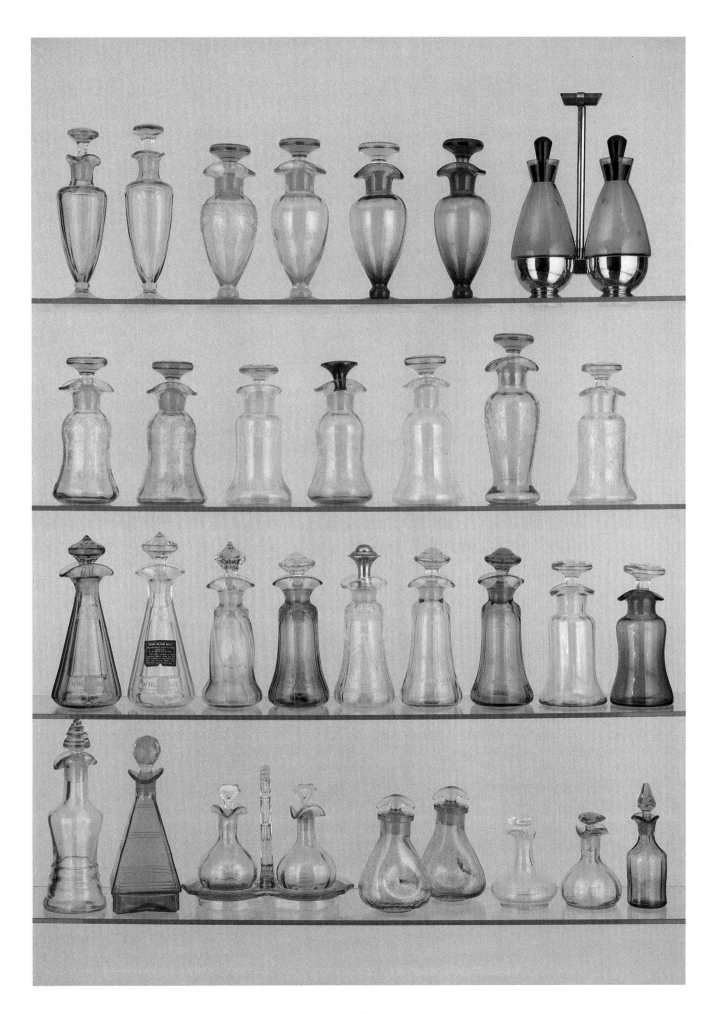

REAMERS — BABY

I have had more letters about reamers since the last book than any other subject. The Barnes reamer shown in Row 2 was only the beginning of the repros. Unfortunately, original molds were bought after Westmoreland's demise and used to make these reproductions. The Barnes reamers are marked with B in a circle. However, Summit Art Glass of Akron, Ohio, is using original molds under a private contract without marking the glass in any way!

Other repros have come from Taiwan. See pages 221-223 for Reproductions for a complete run down on reproductions as close to publishing date as possible. Items with an asterisk below have been reproduced. To keep abreast of all the reamer news I suggest you join the national reamer club. The address is as follows: National Reamer Collectors Association, c/o Terry McDuffee, 1478 West Cypress Ave., Redlands, Ca. 92373.

Westmoreland Glass Company (Rows 1-3)

Row 1:	#1	Pink, 2 piece	125.00–150.00
	#2	Same, crystal	75.00– 85.00
	#3	Blue (bottom only $90.00-100.00)	175.00–200.00
	#4	Amber, 2 piece	150.00–200.00
	#5	Sun-colored-amethyst (bottom only $40.00-45.00)	80.00– 90.00
	#6	Green, 2 piece	165.00–200.00
Row 2 & 3:		**Bottom is worth ⅔ of price except where noted below.**	
*Row 2:	#1	Frosted pink	110.00–125.00
	#2	Green (top & bottom about equal in value)	200.00–220.00
	#3	Crystal w/decorations	35.00– 40.00
	#4	Pink (bottom value $20.00-25.00)	95.00–110.00
	#5	Frosted blue bottom only	40.00– 45.00
	#6	Sun-colored-amethyst (SCA)	60.00– 70.00
*Row 3:	#1	Frosted crystal (decorated add $10.00)	50.00– 60.00
	#2	Pink decorated	110.00–125.00
	#3	Blue (bottom value $25.00-30.00)	135.00–155.00
	#4, 5	NEW! RUBINA AND COBALT BLUE MARKED WITH B IN CIRCLE INSIDE CONE OF TOP AND ON BOTTOM OF BASE	
		SEE PAGE 221 FOR ADDITIONAL COLORS.	
Row 4:	#1	L.E. Smith (top rare), pink	225.00–245.00
	#2	Same, green	220.00–250.00
	#3	Same, crystal (in metal add $5.00)	20.00– 30.00
	#4	Jenkins, green	100.00–110.00
	#5	Same, crystal	30.00– 35.00
	#6	Same, frosted crystal	40.00– 45.00
Row 5:	#1	Unknown, blue (top $200.00)	400.00–450.00
	#2	Unknown, pink (top $100.00)	165.00–185.00
	#3	Unknown, crystal (top $10.00)	15.00– 20.00
	#4	Unknown, frosted crystal "Baby's Orange"	65.00– 75.00
	#5	Unknown, crystal	25.00– 35.00
	#6	Unknown, frosted crystal decorated "Baby"	85.00– 95.00
Row 6:	#1	Unknown, crystal	35.00– 40.00
	#2	Unknown, crystal, called "Button & Bows"	45.00– 60.00
	#3	Unknown, crystal probably foreign (emb. sword & hammer)	30.00– 35.00
	#4	Unknown, crystal, "thumbprint" design	45.00– 55.00
	#5	Unknown, crystal, notched top	45.00– 50.00
	#6	Unknown, crystal	30.00– 40.00
Row 7:	#1	Unknown, decorated crystal, "Orange Juice"	55.00– 60.00
	#2	Unknown, frosted decorated crystal	85.00–100.00
	#3	Unknown, pink (possibly foreign)	125.00–150.00
	#4	Fenton, SCA (sun-colored-amethyst) (bottom $55.00)	70.00– 80.00
	#5	Fenton, elephant decorated base	65.00– 75.00

REAMERS – Fenton, Fry, Foreign, Federal and Indiana

The following three pages show the vast price ranges reamer collectors face. Reamers come in all shapes, sizes or colors. The names in quotes with the Fry reamers are the Company names for each color.

The foreign reamers on page 134 represent a separate collecting field in themselves. There are many unique shapes and colors to attract a collector of these reamers made outside the United States.

Page 133

Row	#	Description	Price
Row 1:	#1	Fenton pitcher & reamer set, red	800.00–1,000.00
		(top is ⅓ price; bottom is ⅔ on these)	
	#2	Same, black	800.00–1,000.00
	#3	Same, blue	1,250.00–1,500.00
	#4	Same, jade	550.00– 650.00
Row 2:	#1	Same, transparent green, top only	200.00– 225.00
	#2	Fry, straight side, "Azure" blue	1,250.00–1,500.00
	#3	Same, light green	18.00– 20.00
	#4	Same, "Emerald" green	25.00– 30.00
Row 3:	#1	Same, "Pearl" opalescent white	18.00– 22.00

Row	#	Description	Price
Row 3:		(Continued)	
		Same, embossed "Blue Goose"	175.00–200.00
	#2	Same, "Canary" vaseline	40.00– 45.00
	#3	Same, "Rose" pink	40.00– 55.00
Row 4:	#1	Same, crystal	10.00– 12.50
	#2	Same, "Amber"	300.00–325.00
	#3	Same, "China" white	600.00–800.00
Row 5:	#1	Fry, fluted reamer (jello mold) "Canary"	200.00–225.00
	#2	Same, "Emerald" green	350.00–400.00
	#3	Same, "Rose"	135.00–150.00
Row 6:	#1	Same, "Pearl"	30.00– 35.00
	#2, 3	Tufglas, light or dark	60.00– 75.00

Foreign Reamers
Page 134

Row	#	Description	Price
Row 1:	#1	Pinkish amber	40.00– 45.00
	#2, 5	Cobalt blue or amber	100.00–110.00
	#3	Smoke	75.00– 85.00
	#4	Yellowish custard	90.00–100.00
Row 2:	#1, 5	Pink or light pinkish amber	40.00– 50.00
	#2, 3	Embossed "Foreign," 2 piece, green or pink	40.00– 50.00
	#4	Yellow	125.00–140.00
Row 3:	#1, 3, 5	Root Beer, blue & light yellow, ea.	100.00–110.00
	#2	Embossed "Tcheco-Scovaquie" on handle, crystal	40.00– 50.00
	#4	Embossed sword & hammer on handle	15.00– 20.00
Row 4:	#1, 5	Crystal, last has "K" inside shield mark, ea.	15.00– 20.00
	#2	Light yellow top only	65.00– 75.00
	#3, 4	Pink or "Coke" bottle green	40.00– 55.00

Row	#	Description	Price
Row 5:	#1, 2, 4 & 5	Light green, amber, amethyst or pinkish amber, ea.	60.00– 70.00
	#3	Crystal	25.00– 30.00
Row 6:	#1	Light turquoise	50.00– 55.00
	#2	Green, marked "Argentina"	125.00–135.00
	#3, 5	Cornflower blue or light green	100.00–110.00
	#4	Crystal, embossed fruit	50.00– 60.00
Row 7:	#1, 2	Crystal Czechoslovakia or pink	40.00– 50.00
	#3, 4	Light turquoise or diamond shaped crystal (Rb No 517385)	35.00– 40.00
	#5	Pink	90.00–100.00
	#6	Amber	90.00–110.00

Page 135
Rows 1-3 Federal Glass Company

Row	#	Description	Price
Row 1:	#1	Ribbed, loop handle, pink	22.50–25.00
	#2	Same, amber	17.50–20.00
	#3	Panelled, loop handle, green	22.50–25.00
Row 2:	#1	Same, amber	17.50–20.00
	#2	Tab handle, yellowish/-amber	275.00–300.00
	#3	Same, green	10.00–12.00
	#4	Tab handled, ribbed, seed dam, green	12.50–15.00
Row 3:	#1	Same, pink	85.00–100.00
	#2, 3	Tab handled amber, ea.	10.00–12.50
	#4	Green, pointed cone	12.50–15.00

Row	#	Description	Price
Row 4:	#1	Amber, handled, spout opposite	150.00–200.00
	#2	Same, crystal	12.00–15.00
	#3	Same, pink	40.00–50.00
Row 5:	#1	Same, green	28.00–32.00
	#2	Crystal, horizontal handle	10.00–12.50
	#3	Same, green	12.50–15.00
Row 6:	#1	Crystal, emb. ASCO, "Good Morning, Orange Juice"	18.00–20.00
	#2	Amber, six sided cone, vertical handle	200.00–250.00
	#3	Same, green	25.00–30.00
	#4	Same, pink	100.00–125.00

Rows 4-6 **Indiana Glass Company**

REAMERS — Hazel Atlas and Hocking Glass Companies

The Hazel Atlas 2-cup reamer pitcher has been the plague of novice collectors and dealers for over a year. This has been made in cobalt blue, pink and an odd green color. **See Reproduction Section on pages 221-223** for items with asterisk.

Page 137 All Hazel Atlas Glass Company

Row 1:	#1	Yellow 2 cup pitcher and reamer set	250.00–275.00
	#2	Same, cobalt blue	*200.00–250.00
	#3	Same, pink	*110.00–125.00
	#4	Same, green	*22.00– 25.00
Row 2:	#1	Crisscross, cobalt blue	200.00–225.00
	#2	Same, pink	175.00–200.00
	#3	Same, crystal	5.00– 8.00
	#4	Same, green	10.00– 12.00
Row 3:	#1	Green, tab handled	6.50– 7.50
	#2, 3	Decorated 2 cup sets, ea.	30.00– 35.00
	#4	Fired-on red set	45.00– 50.00
Row 4:	#1, 3-5	Decorated sets, ea.	30.00– 35.00
	#2	Tumbler to match #1	6.00– 8.00
Row 5:	#1	Crisscross, tab handled, pink	225.00–275.00
	#2	Same, green	9.00– 11.00
	#3	Same, crystal	3.00– 5.00
	#4	Green, tab handled	6.50– 7.50

Page 138 All Hazel Atlas Glass Company

Row 1:	#1	Reamer pit., 4 cup marked A&J, green	30.00– 35.00
	#2	Same, A & J, Pat Applied For, crystal	18.00– 20.00
	#3	Green, 4 cup, ftd.	30.00– 35.00
	#4	Green, stippled pitcher	30.00– 35.00
Row 2:	#1, 2	Tab handle, lemon, pink, light or dark	25.00– 35.00
	#3	Same, green	12.00– 15.00
	#4	Same, white w/red trim	22.50– 25.00
Row 3:	#1-3	White, w/decorated trim, 4 cup	30.00– 35.00
	#4	White, 4 cup, stippled pitcher	27.50– 32.50
Row 4:	#1	Small tab handled reamer, pink	35.00– 40.00
	#2	Same, green	12.00– 15.00
	#3	Same, cobalt blue	250.00–300.00
	#4	Large tab handled reamer, pink	27.50– 30.00
Row 5:	#1	Same, white	35.00– 40.00
	#2	Same, cobalt blue	225.00–250.00
	#3	Same, crystal	4.50– 5.00
	#4	Same, green	12.00– 15.00

Page 139 All Hocking or Anchor Hocking Glass Company

Row 1:	#1	"Circle" pitcher w/reamer top	60.00– 65.00
	#2	Pitcher reamer, 4 cup, ftd., green	30.00– 35.00
	#3	Pitcher reamer, 4 cup, flat, green	22.00– 25.00
Row 2:	#1	Pitcher reamer, 2 cup, green	20.00– 22.50
	#2	Same, Vitrock	25.00– 30.00
	#3	Pitcher reamer, ribbed, 2 cup	50.00– 55.00
	#4	Same, crystal	20.00– 22.50
Row 3:	#1	Pitcher reamer, 4 cup, crystal	20.00– 25.00
	#2	Vitrock, tab	75.00– 95.00
	#3	Green "Clambroth," tab	90.00–115.00
	#4	Pitcher top, "Mayfair blue"	200.00–250.00
Row 4:	#1-3	Orange reamer, loop handle, green, ea.	12.50– 15.00
Row 5:	#1	Same, Vitrock	18.00– 20.00
	#2	Fired-on black tab	10.00– 12.50
	#3	Green tab	10.00– 12.00

REAMERS — Fleur-de-Lis, Jeannette and Miscellaneous

The reamers shown on Page 141 are found mostly on the West coast. I am amazed at the variety of shades of opaque red found on Fleur-de-Lis reamers. There is a fleur-de-lis emblem embossed on the side of most of these. (If not, it is listed as unembossed). The opalescent red shades are quite beautiful particularly when they are displayed in a lighted cabinet.

There are price differences caused by color variations, whether there are emblems or not and whether the reamers possess rims or not.

Note the large Delphite reamer Row 3, #4 on Page 143. There have been few of these found!

See **Reproduction Section on pages 221-223** for items with asterisk.

Page 141

Row 1:	#1	"VALENCIA," white (embossed word)	90.00–100.00
	#2	Same, crystal	150.00–200.00
	#3	Same, green	175.00–200.00
Row 2:	#1	Plain, no embossing, "VALENCIA"	75.00– 85.00
	#2	Same, opalescent white	50.00– 60.00
	#3	Same, pink	150.00–200.00
	#4	Same, pinkish amber	175.00–225.00
Row 3:	#1, 4	"Fleur-de-Lis," red/orange slag	350.00–425.00
	#2	Same, amberina/opalescent	550.00–650.00
	#3	Same, mustard/slag	375.00–450.00

Row 4:	#1	Embossed white "Fleur-de-Lis"	75.00– 85.00
	#2	Same, red/orange slag	350.00–425.00
	#3	Same, red	425.00–500.00
	#4	Same, root beer	550.00–600.00
Row 5:	#1	Same, crystal	175.00–200.00
	#2	Unembossed, grayish custard	125.00–150.00
	#3	Same, custard w/"rim edge"	135.00–150.00
	#4	Same, white w/"rim edge"	40.00– 60.00
Row 6:	#1	"LINDSAY," pink	375.00–425.00
	#2	"LINDSEY," pink	375.00–425.00
	#3	"LINDSAY," green	400.00–450.00

Page 142

Row 1:	#1	Large crystal (called "monster")	25.00– 35.00
	#2	Light turquoise, O J extractor	100.00–125.00
	#3	Foreign, pink	65.00– 75.00
	#4	Crystal, Glasbake, McKee on handle	80.00–125.00
Row 2:	#1	Hazel Atlas old reamer (recently iridized)	50.00– 60.00
	#2	Green "log" handle	100.00–125.00
	#3	Crystal	10.00– 12.50
	#4	"Colony" like, twin spout	*15.00– 20.00
		Same, white	150.00–200.00
	#5	Foreign, amber	65.00– 75.00
Row 3:	#1	"Clambroth," "British make," embossed	175.00–200.00
	#2	"MacBeth-Evans Glass Co., Charleroi, Pa."	325.00–350.00
	#3	"Clambroth," boat shaped	150.00–185.00
Row 4:	#1	Black, "Orange Juice Extractor"	300.00–350.00

Row 4: (Continued)			
	#2	Same, green	45.00– 50.00
	#3	Same, pink	80.00– 90.00
	#4	Same, "Clambroth"	85.00–100.00
Row 5:	#1	Green, like #2, but unembossed	150.00–200.00
	#2	Crystal, embossed "Sunkist Oranges & Lemons" or "Los Angeles Fruit Growers Exchange," ea.	25.00– 35.00
	#3	Pink, unembossed	185.00–200.00
Row 6:	#1	Crystal, square, marked Italy	12.50– 15.00
	#2	"Easley's," (called "chisel cone")	65.00– 75.00
	#3	"Easley's," square opalescent white	150.00–175.00
	#4	"Read," some embossed, some not	100.00–125.00
	#5	Unusual six sided top	45.00– 50.00

Page 143 All Jeannette Glass Company

Row 1:	#1	"Hex Optic" bucket reamer, pink	40.00–45.00
	#2	Same, green	35.00–40.00
	#3	2 cup reamer pitcher	90.00–110.00
	#4	Same, w/top (see page 24)	1,000.00–1,200.00
Row 2:	#1	Crystal, large, loop handle	8.00–10.00
	#2	Same, green	15.00–20.00
	#3	2 cup reamer pitcher, light Jadite	15.00–20.00
	#4	Same, dark Jadite matching top/bottom	60.00–100.00
Row 3:	#1	Small, Delphite	55.00–65.00
	#2	Large, dark Jadite	20.00–25.00

Row 3: (Continued)			
	#3	Same, light Jadite	18.00–20.00
	#4	Same, Delphite	900.00–1,000.00
Row 4:	#1	Small, dark Jadite	22.00–25.00
	#2	Same, light Jadite	20.00–22.00
	#3	"Jennyware," crystal	60.00–75.00
	#4	Same, pink	60.00–70.00
	#5	Same, ultra-marine	70.00–80.00
Row 5:	#1	Green, 5" tab reamer	12.00–15.00
	#2	Green, 5⅞" tab reamer	12.50–15.00
	#3	Same as #1, crystal	8.00–10.00
	#4	Same as #2, pink	35.00–40.00
	#5	Same as #1, pink	35.00–40.00

REAMERS - Cambridge and McKee

McKee Glass Company made most of the Sunkist reamers, though not all. The McKee symbol is an "McK" with a circle around it and said insignia adds interest to a reamer. Collectors of reamers concern themselves with color, type (lemon, orange, grapefruit), handles, spouts, seed dams or no, footed or flat bottomed, embossing, size and shape of the reaming section, etc. As usual, scarcity and demand determines price for reamers, many of which are not cheap!

Page 145

Row 1: #1 Cambridge green 175.00– 200.00
#2, 3 Same, light pink 175.00– 200.00
Row 2: #1 Same, amber 600.00– 700.00
#2 Same, green w/silver Rockwell decoration 300.00– 350.00
#3 Cambridge, crystal 20.00– 25.00
Same, Cobalt blue (shown page 21) 2,000.00–2,500.00
Row 3: #1 Cambridge, small tab, crystal 12.50– 15.00
#2 Same, cobalt blue 250.00– 300.00
#3 Cambridge, small, ftd., green 300.00– 400.00
Same, crystal, (not shown) 12.00– 15.00

Row 3: (Continued)
Same, pink, (not shown) 300.00–350.00
Same, cobalt blue, (not shown) 750.00–850.00
#4 Grapefruit, ultra-marine 400.00–450.00
Row 4: #1 Same, Seville yellow 180.00–210.00
#2 Same, flat yellow 225.00–250.00
#3 Same, custard 300.00–350.00
Row 5: #1 Same, "Caramel" 650.00–750.00
#2 Same, black 750.00–850.00
#3 Same, white 250.00–350.00
Row 6: #1 Same, Jadite 110.00–135.00
#2 Same, Chalaine blue 350.00–450.00
#3 Same, pink 500.00–600.00

Page 146 All embossed "SUNKIST" unless noted.

Row 1: #1 Green opalescent "fry" 110.00–175.00
#2 Opalescent "fry" 75.00– 85.00
#3 Transparent ultra-marine 500.00–600.00
#4 Butterscotch "fry" 500.00–600.00
Row 2: #1 Lilac pinkish white 50.00– 60.00
#2 Pink 40.00– 50.00
#3 Light pink 50.00– 65.00
#4 Pinkish amber 100.00–150.00
Row 3: #1 "Blocked" letters in "SUNKIST," swirl 250.00–300.00
#2 Black 400.00–450.00
#3 Chalaine blue 145.00–165.00
#4 Chocolate 300.00–500.00
Row 4: #1 Turquoise blue milk glass 250.00–350.00

Row 4: (Continued)
#2 Jadite 18.00– 20.00
#3 Dark Jadite, slightly opalescent 100.00–125.00
#4 Olive green milk glass 500.00–600.00
Row 5: #1 Transparent green 40.00– 45.00
#2 Unembossed green 200.00–250.00
#3 Forest Green 350.00–400.00
#4 Vaseline green 30.00– 35.00
Row 6: #1 Seville yellow 35.00– 40.00
#2 Yellowish custard 30.00– 35.00
#3 Custard 25.00– 30.00
#4 Greenish custard 55.00– 60.00

Page 147 "SUNKIST" Rows 1-3

Row 1: #1 Ivory 125.00–150.00
#2 Gray 135.00–150.00
#3 Opal white (value determined by opalescence) 35.00–100.00
#4 White 7.00– 10.00
Row 2: #1 "Blocked" letters in "SUNKIST," white 55.00– 75.00
#2 Opal Crown Tuscan 200.00–250.00
#3 Crown Tuscan milk glass 200.00–250.00
#4 Caramel variation 200.00–250.00
Row 3: #1 Caramel, light 200.00–250.00
#2 Caramel, medium 250.00–300.00
#3 Caramel, butterscotch 250.00–300.00
#4 Mustard 300.00–350.00
Row 4: #1 Skokie Green, pointed cone, 5¼" 50.00– 55.00

Row 4: (Continued)
#2 Same, Custard 45.00– 50.00
#3 Jadite, unembossed, smaller foot than embossed below in Row 6 18.00– 20.00
Row 5: #1 White, "McK" embossed 18.00– 20.00
#2 Same, Custard 18.00– 20.00
#3 Same, Jadite 18.00– 20.00
#4 Same, Delphite 225.00–275.00
Row 6: #1 White, 6", "McK" embossed 45.00– 60.00
#2 Same, Custard w/red trim 35.00– 40.00
#3 Same, Jadite 25.00– 28.00
#4 Same, Delphite 300.00–350.00

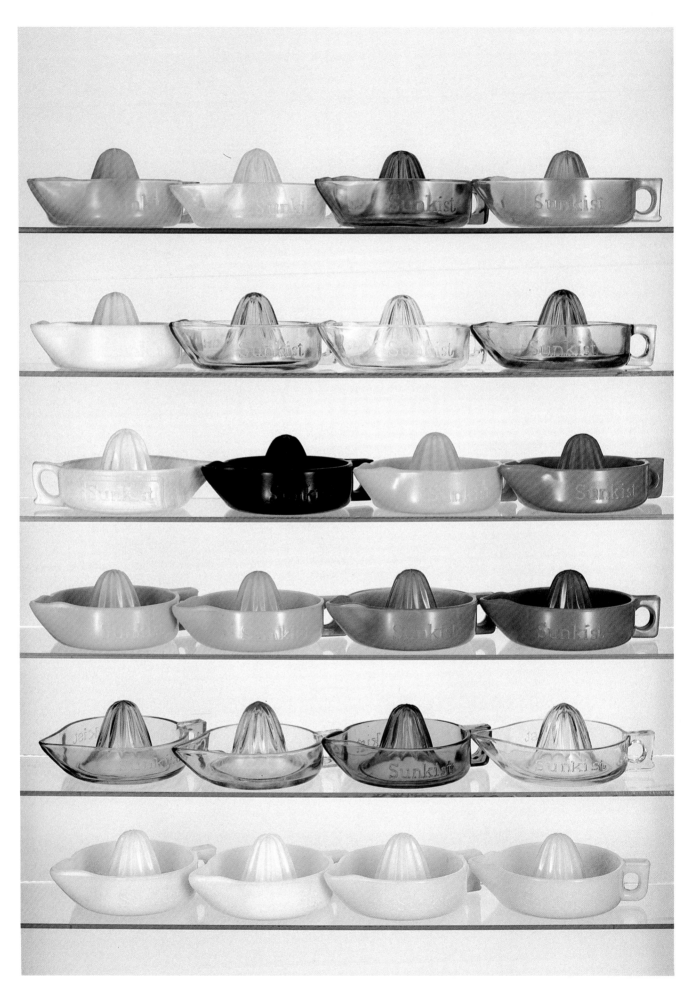

REAMERS - Paden City, Westmoreland and U.S. Glass Companies

There are numerous cocktail shaker bottoms missing their reamer tops. That reamer top is a hard to find item, so don't buy too many topless shakers. There are no replacements for these available. **See Reproduction Section pages 221-223** for items with asterisk.

There are several different inserts for the U.S. Glass reamers. The pitcher in Row 1, #1 and the tubs in Row 2 on Page 150 each have a 4½" diameter reamer top. A 4⅛" top fits the other pitchers on Page 150 and the slick handled, horizontal ribbed two cup pitchers on that page. The same 4⅛" top fits all the loop handled two cup pitchers on Page 151. The insert for the four cup pitchers is 5⅛" in diameter.

Page 149

Row 1:	#1	Pink cocktail shaker/ reamer, "Party Line"	75.00– 85.00
	#2	Same, amber	85.00– 95.00
	#3	Green, cocktail shaker/ reamer, "Speakeasy"	35.00– 40.00
	#4	Pink pitcher and reamer top	150.00–200.00
		Same, crystal pitcher w/black handle & top (shown page 155	250.00–300.00
	#5	Green, 4 cup pitcher & top, "Party Line"	100.00–125.00
Row 2:	#1	Same, pink	125.00–150.00
	#2	Same, crystal complete	65.00– 75.00
		Same, turquoise blue complete	250.00–300.00
		Same, black (shown page 155)	450.00–500.00

Row 2:	(Continued)		
	#3	Westmoreland, green, 2 piece, embossed orange/lemon	*125.00–150.00
	#4	Same, pink	*125.00–150.00
Row 3:	#1	Same, crystal	*150.00–175.00
	#2, 3	Westmoreland, crystal decorated oranges or lemons, flattened loop handle, ea	*75.00– 90.00
Row 4:	#1	Same, dark green	*90.00–125.00
	#2	Same, light green	*90.00–125.00
	#3	Same, bluish green	*125.00–140.00
Row 5:	#1	Same, white	*200.00–250.00
	#2	Same, pink	*75.00– 85.00
	#3	Same, amber	*200.00–250.00

Page 150 All U.S. Glass Company

Row 1:	#1, 4	Reamer pitcher set, 3 piece, pink, ea.	225.00–250.00
	#2	Reamer pitcher set, green	200.00–250.00
		Same, yellow, shown on page 79	650.00–750.00
	#3	Tumbler for set	10.00– 12.50
Row 2:	#1	Tub, w/reamer top, pink	150.00–200.00
	#2	Same, green	150.00–200.00
	#3	"Vidrio Products No. J - 50"	150.00–165.00
	#4	Slick handle, 2 piece, horizontal ribs, (each rib is ½ cup) amber	200.00–300.00
Row 3:	#1	Slick handle, green, insert near top of cup (graduated measurements on side	30.00– 35.00

Row 3:	(Continued)		
	#2	Same, pink	30.00– 35.00
	#3	Same as Row 2, #4, pink	28.00– 32.00
	#4	Same, frosted pink	30.00– 33.00
Row 4:	#1	Same, green	30.00– 35.00
	#2	Same, turquoise blue	85.00–100.00
	#3	Same, crystal	20.00– 22.50
	#4	Same, frosted green	25.00– 28.00
Row 5:	#1	Slick handle, barred or vertical ribs	40.00– 50.00
	#2	"Handy Andy," green (note reamer cone differs)	40.00– 50.00
	#3	Crystal, same as #1	15.00– 18.00

Page 151 All U.S. Glass Company

Row 1:	#1	4 cup pitcher set, amber	400.00–500.00
	#2	Same, green	85.00–110.00
	#3	Same, pink	200.00–250.00
Row 2:	#1	2 cup, pitcher set, light pink	35.00– 40.00
	#2	Same, dark pink	35.00– 40.00
	#3	Same, white	125.00–150.00
	#4	Same, amber	250.00–300.00
Row 3:	#1	Same, yellow (light honey amber)	250.00–300.00
	#2	Same, blue complete	500.00–600.00
		Same, crystal, complete	15.00– 17.50
	#3, 5	Same, crystal, decorated, ea.	20.00– 25.00
	#4	Tumbler, matching reamer	5.00– 7.50

Row 4:	#1	Same, frosted green	30.00– 32.50
	#2	Same, bluish green (turquoise)	100.00–115.00
	#3	Same, dark green	35.00– 40.00
	#4	Same, light green	30.00– 35.00
Row 5:	#1	Slick handle, light pink	85.00–100.00
	#2	Same, dark pink	90.00–110.00
	#3	Same, amber	250.00–300.00
Row 6:	#1	Same, white	50.00– 60.00
	#2	Same, green	55.00– 65.00
	#3	Slick handle, grapefruit	300.00–350.00

REAMERS - Miscellaneous, Mechanical and Unusual

This is the "catch-all" section on reamers. Reamers not fitting previous categories go on these pages. Most of the glass manufactures are unknown, although I still feel sure that McKee made the Saunders and possibly the Radnt. No valid catalogue information has ever surfaced!

One of the reamers I find most fascinating is the RE-GO shown in Rows 3 and 5 on page 153. I find it unbelievable that these ever survived being used. It is a mechanical, glass, two part reamer. The only thing separating the glass from crunching together is a small wooden peg which allows the insert to be turned by hand to extract the juice.

The name RE-GO comes from a reamer that originally said "puRE-GOld." (The small letters in pure gold were placed there for emphasis by me.) The PURE-GOLD reamer itself may never have been marketed; the first name was altered by removing the letters "p,u,l,d" to leave the name RE-GO. The old letters can still be seen on these reamers, albeit slightly.

The green insert shown in Row 3 #1 is called "EASY SQUEEZE" and is used on a similar base as that of the RE-GO.

The crystal pitcher on Page 155 in Row 2, #3 has to have a **black handle** for price listed.

Page 153

Row 1:	#1	Jadite, embossed SAUNDERS	700.00– 800.00
	#2	"Sanitary Bess Mixer", (embossed **"4"** inside a large **"1"**)	175.00– 200.00
	#3	"Ideal" Pat'd Jan 31, 1888	125.00– 175.00
	#4	Black, same as #1	750.00– 850.00
Row 2:	#1	"Tricia", black	800.00–1,000.00
	#2	Same, pink complete	450.00– 550.00
		Same, crystal complete	300.00– 350.00
	#3	Same, green	400.00– 500.00
Row 3:	#1	"EASY SQUEEZE", green top only	200.00– 250.00
		Same, complete (not shown)	500.00– 550.00
	#2	Green RE-GO	400.00– 500.00
	#3	RE-GO crystal top only	125.00– 150.00
		Same, complete (not shown)	300.00– 400.00
Row 4:	#1	"RADNT", crystal	95.00– 115.00
	#2	Same, green	300.00– 400.00
	#3	Same, pink	300.00– 400.00
Row 5:	#1	RE-GO, opalescent white	550.00– 650.00
	#2	Same, blue	1000.00–1,250.00
	#3	Same, black (top shown)	1000.00–1,250.00

Page 154

Row 1:	#1	Metal insert	40.00– 45.00
	#2	Glass insert, probably Hocking	175.00–225.00
	#3	Mount Joy	125.00–150.00
Row 2:	#1	"Mayfair" blue glass insert, probably Hocking	250.00–300.00
	#2	"SUNKIST" bowl, pink	200.00–250.00

Page 155

Row 1:	#1	Hocking "Mayfair" blue 2 cup reamer pitcher	750.00–1,000.00
Row 2:	#1	Paden City "Party Line", black	450.00– 500.00
	#2	Paden City, green	200.00– 250.00
	#3	Paden City, crystal pitcher, black handle & top	250.00– 300.00

REFRIGERATOR CONTAINERS

Page 157

Row 1:	#1	Pyrex, 4¼" x 6¾", blue & white ($4.00-5.00); blue	12.00–15.00
	#2	Same, 3½" x 4¾", blue & white ($2.00-3.00); blue	8.00–10.00
	#3	Same, red ($4.00-5.00); crystal "Crosley Shelvador"	4.00– 5.00
	#4	Green, 5" x 5", leaf design, U.S. Glass Co.	12.50–15.00
Row 2:	#1	Federal, pink 4" x 4" ($6.00-8.00); 4" x 8" ($18.00-20.00); 8" x 8"	30.00–32.00
	#2	Same, 4½" round, pink ($12.00-15.00); white 5½" round	6.00– 8.00
	#3	Same, 4½" round, amber ($6.00-8.00); 8" x 8" ($12.00-14.00); 4" x 4"	6.00– 8.00

Hazel Atlas Glass Company

Row 3:	#1	5¾" round, flat knob, green ($20.00-22.00); cobalt blue	50.00–60.00
	#2	5¾" round, pointed knob, decorated	12.00–15.00
	#3	Same as #1, white	10.00–12.00
	#4	5" round, white w/green leaf	6.00– 8.00
Row 4:	#1	"Crisscross," blue, 4" x 4" ($22.50-25.00); 4" x 8" ($55.00-60.00); 8" x 8"	75.00–85.00
	#2	Same, 3½" x 5¾", crystal ($12.00-15.00); green	35.00–45.00
	#3	Same, 5¼" round, pink	75.00–85.00
	#4	4½" x 5" pink ($25.00-30.00); yellow ($30.00-35.00); green ($20.00-22.00); blue	40.00–45.00

Page 158

Row 1:	#1	Fry, 4½" x 8"	25.00–30.00
	#2	Glassbake, 4¼" square, light blue	3.00– 4.00
	#3	Same, 4½" x 5", crystal	8.00–10.00
	#4	Green Clambroth, 3⅝" square	6.00– 8.00
Row 2:	#1	McKee, 4" x 5" red "Dots" ($12.50-15.00); Delphite ($22.50-25.00); blue "Dots," 5" x 8"	18.00–20.00
	#2	5" x 8" Chalaine blue ($55.00–65.00) 4" x 5" Custard or Seville	12.00–15.00
	#3	5" x 8" Seville yellow ($18.00-22.00); 4" x 5" Jadite ($12.00-14.00); Chalaine	35.00–45.00
Row 3:	#1	Seville yellow, 7¼" square	30.00–35.00
	#2	Crystal, 3½" x 5½"	12.00–15.00
	#3	Jadite, 4¼" beater bowl	6.00– 7.00
	#4	Jadite, 10 oz. canister	11.00–13.00

Hocking Glass Company

Row 4:	#1	4¼" x 4¾", 2 styles, green, ea.	18.00–20.00
	#2	Same, green Clambroth	20.00–22.50
	#3	6" square, green	18.00–20.00
	#4	"Fire-King," 4" x 4⅛"	4.00– 5.00
Row 5:	#1	8" x 8", Vitrock ($22.00-25.00); 4" x 4", Vitrock ($8.00-10.00); green, ea.	10.00–12.00
	#2	"Fire-King" Jad-ite, 4½" x 5¼" ($6.00-8.00); 5" x 9"	10.00–12.00
	#3	Same, blue, 4½" x 5"	7.00– 9.00
	#4	Oval, 8" green ($22.00-25.00); 7" fired-on blue ($15.00-18.00); 6" green Clambroth	15.00–18.00

Page 159

Row 1:	#1	"Jennyware" 16 oz. round	18.00–20.00
	#2	Glassbake, 5½" square w/lid	18.00–20.00
	#3, 4	McKee Hall's, 4" x 5" or 4" x 6" ea.	10.00–14.00

Jeannette Glass Company

Row 2:	#1	Floral, 5" x 5", Jadite ($18.00-20.00); 5" x 10"	28.00–30.00
	#2	4" x 4" Jadite ($11.00-13.00); Delphite	20.00–25.00
	#3	4" x 8" Jadite ($15.00-18.00); Delphite	30.00–35.00
Row 3:	#1	Floral, 5" x 5" green	45.00–55.00
	#2, 3	Round dish, 32 oz., Jadite ($22.00-25.00); Delphite	35.00–40.00
	#4	Round crock, 40 oz., Jadite	38.00–40.00
Row 4:	#1	"Kompakt," green, 4" x 4" ($15.00-17.00); 4" x 8" (not shown)	32.50–37.50
		Same, SCA, 4" x 8"	12.00–14.00
	#2	Jennyware, 4½" square pink ($18.00-20.00); ultra-marine	20.00–22.00
	#3	Same, 4½" x 9", pink ($25.00-28.00); ultra-marine	27.00–30.00
Row 5:	#1	"Hex Optic," 6" round base ($12.00-15.00); lid ($8.00-10.00); 3 piece	30.00–35.00
	#2	Same, 4½" x 5", green, base ($8.00-10.00); lid ($10.00-12.00); 3 piece	26.00–32.00
	#3	Radnt jar, 5" lid & 5½" tall	18.00–22.00
	#4	Ultra-marine 4" x 4" ($15.00-17.00); 4" x 8"	20.00–25.00

157

ROLLING PINS

The abundance of crystal rolling pins has not noticeably diminished. These sell in the $10.00–12.00 range. Dealers who sell primitives or crafts are filling these with marbles, beans and other colorful things in order to sell them. I saw one around Easter with jelly beans priced at $25.00!

Shown below are some new additions to the listing: black and "Robin Egg" blue. Both of these are the blown type shown on page 163.

Page 160
> Row 1: #1 Black   250.00–300.00
>
> #2 "Robin Egg" blue   300.00–350.00

Page 161 McKee Glass Company except for last row

Row 1:	Note circular band opposite shaker top end.		
	#1	Jadite	225.00–275.00
	#2	Custard	150.00–175.00
Row 2 & 3:	Note smooth end opposite shaker top end on these rows.		
	#1	Seville yellow	200.00–225.00
	#2	Delphite blue	325.00–375.00
Row 3:	#1	Chalaine blue	350.00–400.00
	#2	Jadite	250.00–275.00
Row 4:	#1	Crystal w/screw-on cobalt handles	175.00–200.00

Wooden Handles
Page 162

Row 1:		Peacock blue (handles attached to metal rod inside pin)	150.00–200.00
Row 2:	#1	Green transparent (handles attached to wood dowel pin)	275.00–325.00
	#2	Pink (screw-on wooden handles)	275.00–325.00
Row 3:	#1	White (comes w/wood or metal screw-on handles), ea. marked "Imperial Mfg. Co., Cambridge, Ohio"	35.00– 44.00
		Same, Custard color (not shown)	140.00–165.00
	#2	Cobalt blue (handles attached to metal rod inside pin)	300.00–350.00
Row 4:		Clambroth white (screw-on wood handles)	75.00– 85.00

Blown Rolling Pins
Page 163

Row 1:	#1	Amethyst	85.00–100.00
	#2	Cobalt blue	150.00–175.00
Row 2:	#1	Amber, light	100.00–110.00
	#2	Forest green	125.00–140.00
Row 3:	#1	Peacock blue, dark	125.00–150.00
	#2	Crystal, "Kardov Flour, Famous Self Rising"	35.00– 45.00
Row 4:	#1	Chalaine blue	275.00–325.00
	#2	Blue, light	150.00–175.00

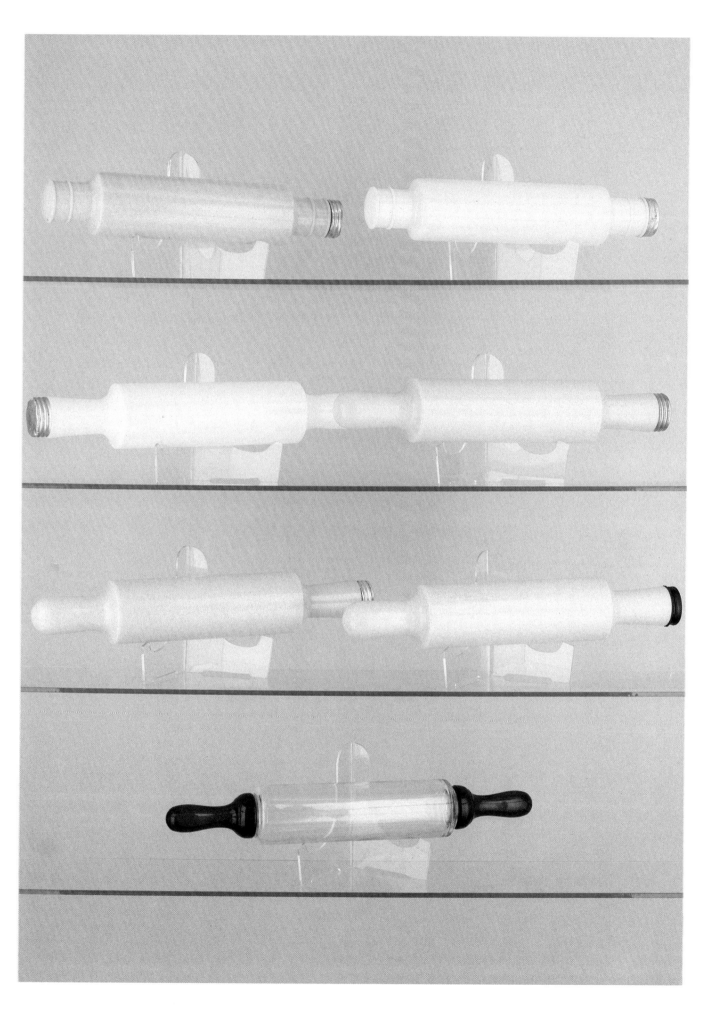

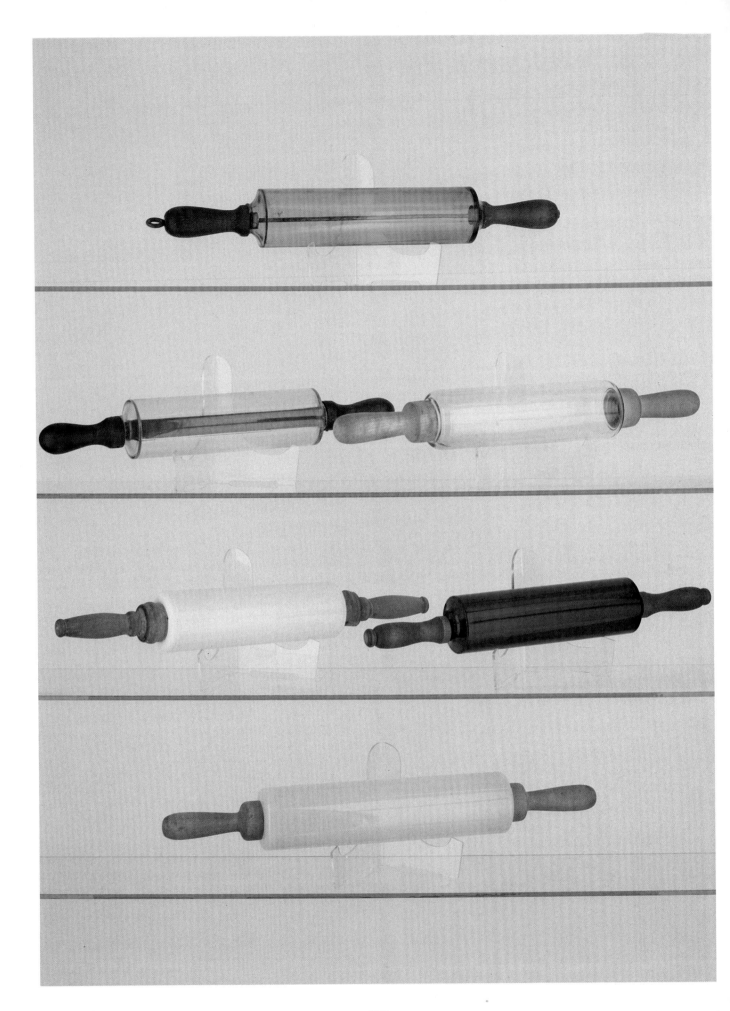

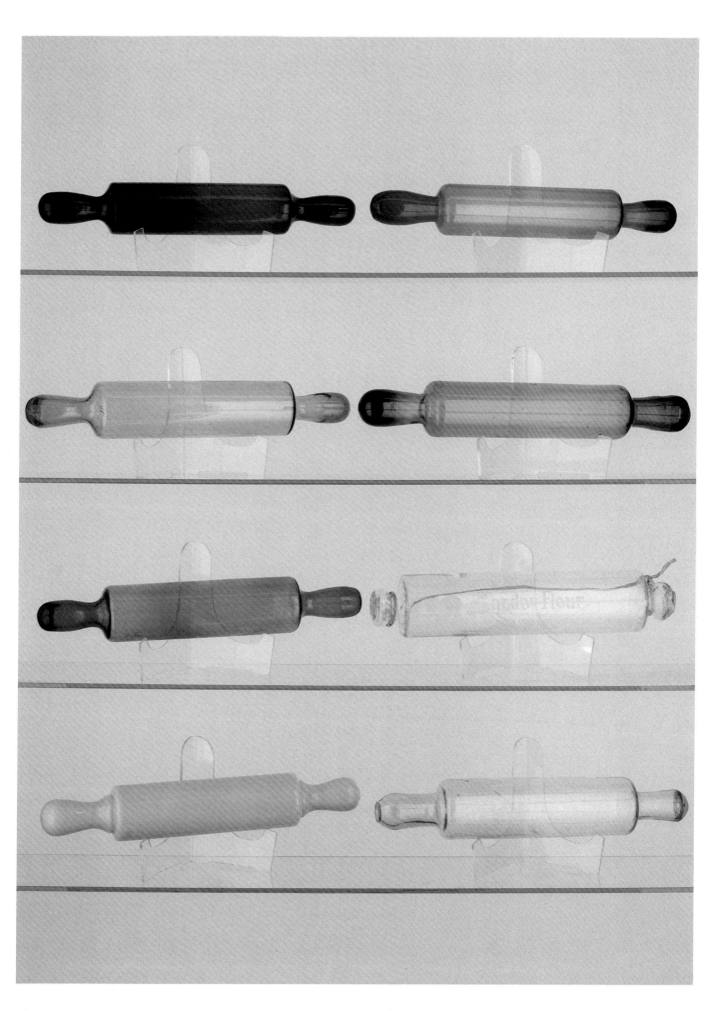

SALAD SETS and Additional LADLES

The inclusion of salad sets in the Kitchen book opened a new collecting field for some buyers who were not aware of the variety available before then. Prices of the colored sets have skyrocketed, especially those from identifiable companies. Many of these sets were of foreign manufacture – mainly Czechoslovakia.

Row 1 on page 167 contains Cambridge salad sets. Besides those shown, cobalt blue is also available. Forks and spoons sell about same price, but there seems to be a small premium ($1.00–5.00) for the set.

A few remaining ladles that would not fit in that section are included on page 167.

Prices below are for sets unless otherwise noted. (Half of lowest price listed for one piece only)

Page 165

Row 1:	#1	Blue, large pointed handle set	50.00–60.00
	#2, 4		
	& 5	Same, amber or green set	30.00–40.00
		Same, pink (not shown) marked "TCHECOBLOV"	40.00–50.00
	#3	Yellow, small pointed handle set	30.00–40.00
	#6-9	Same, peacock or cobalt blue set	55.00–70.00
	#10	Same, red set	75.00–85.00
	#11, 12	Boxed forks, green or pink, ea	20.00–25.00
Row 2:	#1, 2	Long crystal handled amber set	30.00–35.00
	#3, 4	Red teardrop handle set	50.00–60.00
		Same, cobalt blue (not shown)	45.00–55.00
		Same, amethyst (not shown)	40.00–50.00
	#5	Green top and bottom set	40.00–50.00
	#6-8	Blue or green set	50.00–60.00
	#9	Amber flattened stripped handle set	30.00–40.00
Row 3:	#1, 2	Forest green set	40.00–45.00
	#3, 4	Black handled set	55.00–65.00
	#5, 6	All amber set, found with Czechoslovakia labels	40.00–50.00
	#7	White set, serrated and waffle back	40.00–50.00
	#8	Canary yellow or vaseline, set	60.00–70.00

Page 166

Row 1:	#1, 2	Cobalt blue, rounded, ribbed handle set	35.00–45.00
	#3, 4	Same, green	30.00–40.00
	#5, 6	Same, light blue	40.00–50.00
	#7, 8	Same, amber	25.00–35.00
	#9	Same, crystal	17.00–20.00
		Same, pink (not shown)	35.00–40.00
Row 2:	#1	Blue w/crystal top, set	35.00–45.00
	#2, 3	Forest green flattened handle set	45.00–55.00
	#4, 5	Pink set, edge down sides	35.00–45.00
	#6, 7	Same, cobalt blue	40.00–50.00
	#8, 9	Same, amber	30.00–35.00
Row 3:	#1	Blue pointed fork, set	45.00–55.00
	#2-4	Amber or pink flattened handle set	40.00–45.00
	#5, 6	Same, green	45.00–50.00
	#7, 8	Amber set	40.00–45.00
	#9-11	Amber 3 piece set	75.00–90.00
		Same, cake server only	40.00–45.00

Page 167

Row 1:	**All Cambridge Glass Company**		
	#1, 2	Crystal set w/label	35.00– 40.00
	#3-6	Black or light blue	85.00–100.00
	#7, 8	Amber	55.00– 65.00
	#9	Green set	75.00– 85.00
	#10	Red set	125.00–150.00
		Same, cobalt blue (not shown)	150.00–200.00
Row 2:	#1, 2	Light blue set, Imperial (box shown $5.00)	65.00– 75.00
	#3, 4	Same, amber	50.00– 55.00
	#5, 6	Same, green	60.00– 65.00
	#7, 8	Pink set, possibly Imperial	65.00– 75.00
	#9, 10	Same, blue	80.00– 90.00
Row 3:	**Ladles**		
	#1	Green	35.00– 45.00
	#2	Same, crystal	30.00– 35.00
	#3	White, black handle/measure on side of ladle	45.00– 50.00
	#4	Crystal, large	12.00– 15.00

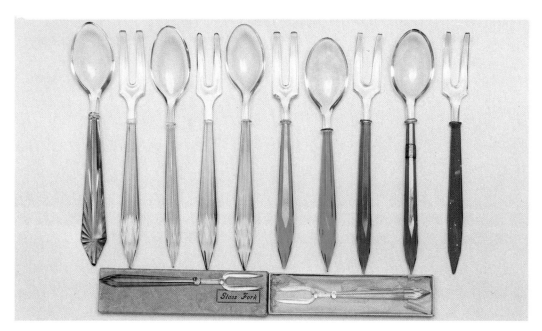

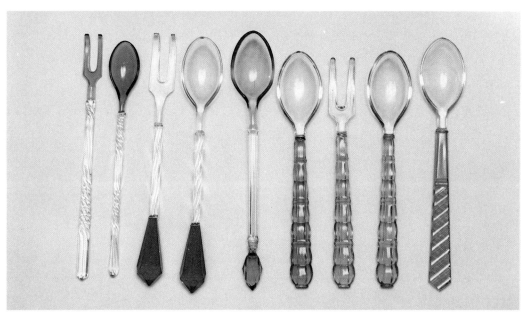

166

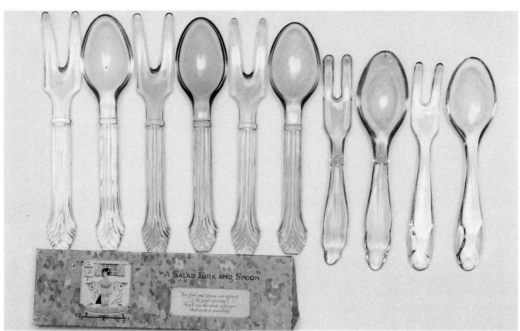

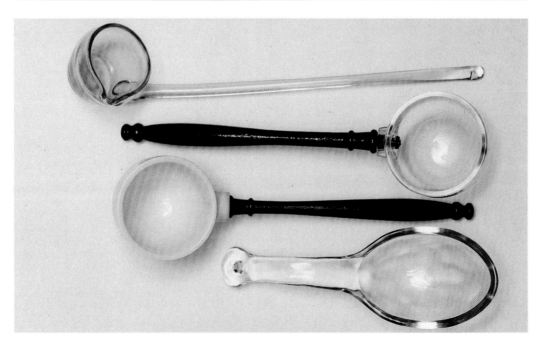

SALT BOXES

Salt boxes are another of the items that few collectors buy per se, but many are bought by collectors of color or by collectors buying sets. The "Zipper" or the "Sneath" cannister sets are not complete without the salts shown here. There is much demand for these latter types and they sell very quickly on the market.

Crystal salt boxes are gathered up by collectors looking to complete "Hoosier" or comparable kitchen cabinet spice and canister sets. I have seen some very high prices on these in shops that sell "primitive" antiques. What I wonder is, "Do they actually get those prices?"

Row 1:	#1	Crystal w/glass lid, embossed SALT, Flintext	80.00– 90.00
	#2	Jadite, Mckee	75.00– 85.00
	#3	Same, Chalaine blue	150.00–175.00
Row 2:	#1	Green "Zipper" w/lid	125.00–150.00
		Same, wo/lid	100.00–125.00
	#2	Peacock blue	125.00–150.00
	#3	Green "Sneath"	175.00–225.00
Row 3:	#1	Jadite w/lid, Jeannette	175.00–195.00
	#2	White, embossed SALT box	100.00–125.00
	#3	White, round embossed SALT box	60.00– 75.00
Row 4:	#1	Crystal, "Sneath"	15.00– 20.00
	#2	Amber "Sneath"	125.00–150.00
	#3	Crystal, embossed SALT	12.00– 15.00
	#4	Crystal, "Zipper"	10.00– 12.00
Row 5:	#1	Green Jeannette round embossed SALT on lid	150.00–165.00
	#2	Crystal salt w/lid	15.00– 17.50
	#3	Crystal, ribbed, embossed SALT	10.00– 12.50
	#4	Crystal, ribbed	8.00– 12.00

SHAKERS, Hocking, Hazel Atlas, Owens Illinois, Tipp City

Be sure to note that the "kitchen cabinet shakers" shown on page 173 Row 4, #5, 6 were actually vacuum cleaner attachments used for blowing moth crystals into your closet.

See Reproduction Section pages 221-223 for items marked with asterisk.

Hocking Glass Company (Rows 1-3)
Page 171

Row 1:	#1-4	Opaque yellow, ea.	10.00–12.00
	#5-7	Fired-on yellow, ea.	4.00– 6.00
	#8-10	Fired-on blue, ea.	10.00–12.00
Row 2:	#1	Fired-on green	7.00– 9.00
	#2, 3	Panelled fired-on blue, ea.	8.00–10.00
	#4-6	Green Clambroth, panelled, ea.	15.00–17.50
	#7, 8	Transparent green, ea.	10.00–12.00
	#9, 10	Vitrock, ea.	5.00– 7.00
Row 3:	#1	Crystal w/raised dots	4.00– 5.00
	#2	Clambroth	8.00–10.00
	#3	Green, plain	9.00–11.00
	#4	Tulip (lid is valued at $1.00-2.00)	4.00– 5.00
	#5, 7 & 8	White, ea.	5.00– 6.00
	#6	Green Jad-ite	4.00– 5.00
	#9	Green, round	20.00–25.00
Row 4:	#1, 2	Hazel Atlas embossed pink salt or pepper	*40.00–50.00
	#3	Same, crystal	20.00–25.00
	#4, 5	Same, green salt or pepper	*25.00–30.00

Row 4:	(Continued)		
	#6, 7	Same, flour or sugar	45.00–60.00
	#8	Dutch salt	10.00–12.50
	#9, 10	White w/green, ea.	6.00– 8.00
Row 5:	#1-4	White w/black, ea.	5.00– 6.00
	#5, 6	Black fired-on, ea.	6.00– 8.00
	#7	Owens-Illinois ovoid shape (good lettering)	9.00–10.00
	#8, 9	Same, square shapes	6.00– 8.00
	#10, 11	Sneath, amber, ea.	22.00–25.00
Row 6:	#1	Crystal, embossed celery	4.00– 5.00
	#2, 3	Crystal, embossed salt & sugar, ea.	5.00– 6.00
	#4	Green, embossed flour	35.00–40.00
	#5	Green	30.00–40.00
	#6	Clambroth	12.00–15.00
	#7	Clambroth	10.00–12.50
	#8	Black, round	15.00–18.00
	#9	Black	8.00–10.00
	#10	Black, ribbed	18.00–20.00

Page 172

Row 1:	#1	Flower, 8 piece set on rack (1 missing here)	20.00–22.50
	#2, 3	Frank Tea & Spice Co., Cincinnati, pr.	10.00–12.50
	#4	Hand painted lady	12.50–15.00
	#5	Griffith's Purified Ground Nutmeg	1.50–2.00
	#6	Decal fruit set on rack (4)	12.00–15.00
Row 2:	#1, 2	Scotty dogs, ea.	6.00–7.50
	#3, 4	Tipp City, ea	2.00–2.50
	#5, 6	Drippings w/salt & pepper set	20.00–25.00
	#7	Green "Moisture Proof" (Nichols Damp Proof Salt Shaker, for 'Pepper also,' Henry Patton Inc., N.Y. N.Y., ea.	50.00–55.00
	#8-11	"Moisture Proof Shakers" (patent 6/25/29) pink or green pr.	110.00–125.00

Row 3:	#1	"Black Circle w/Flowers" grease	18.00–20.00
	#2	"Black Circle" shaker	6.00–7.50
	#3, 4	"Cattail" shakers, ea.	5.00–7.50
	#5	Jadite shaker w/label (Big Hit Allspice-Euclid Coffee Co., Cleveland, Oh.)	10.00–12.50
	#6-8	Hocking white, ea.	5.00–6.00
	#9	Green "Clambroth" handled	20.00–25.00
Row 4:	#1, 3	"Red Flower Pots," ea. w/lid	5.00–6.00
	#2	Same, grease jar	18.00–20.00
	#4	"Blue Circle" shaker	7.50–9.00
	#5, 6	Same, canisters, ea.	18.00–20.00

Page 173

Row 1:	#1, 2	Lady salt or pepper	15.00–17.50
	#3, 4	Same, flour or sugar	17.50–20.00
	#5, 6	Jadite, ea.	10.00–12.50
	#7, 8	"Art Deco," pr.	22.50–25.00
	#9, 10	Blue, pr.	18.00–22.00
	#11, 12	Fired-on blue, pr.	10.00–12.00
Row 2:	#1	Fired-on Dutch set	25.00–30.00
	#2	Dutch white set	12.00–15.00
	#3	Lady watering set (goes with Row 2 on previous page)	25.00–30.00

Row 3:	#1	Singing birds set	20.00–25.00
	#2, 3	Scotty dogs, ea.	6.00– 7.50
	#4	Rooster set	10.00–12.50
	#5, 6	"Sombrero Sam" set	22.00–25.00
	#7, 8	White set w/salt dehumidifier	10.00–12.50
Row 4:	#1, 2	Black set (w/good lettering)	25.00–30.00
	#3, 4	Uncle Sam's hat set	8.00–10.00
	#5, 6	Vacuum cleaner attachments for blowing moth crystals, ea.	12.00–15.00
	#6-9	Floral or cherry, pr.	8.00–10.00

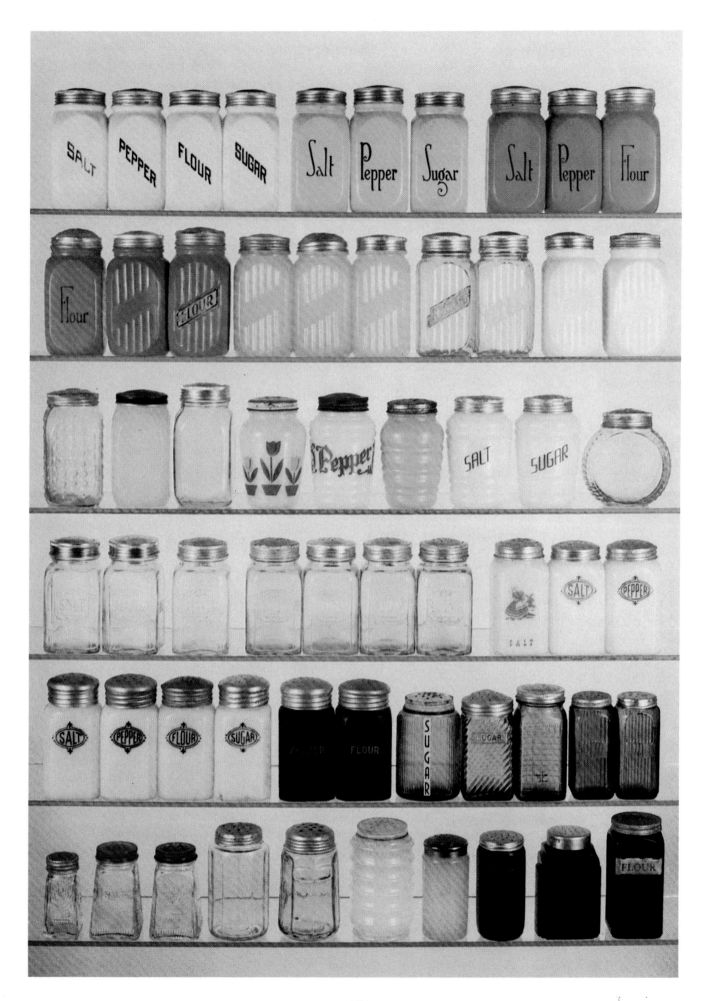

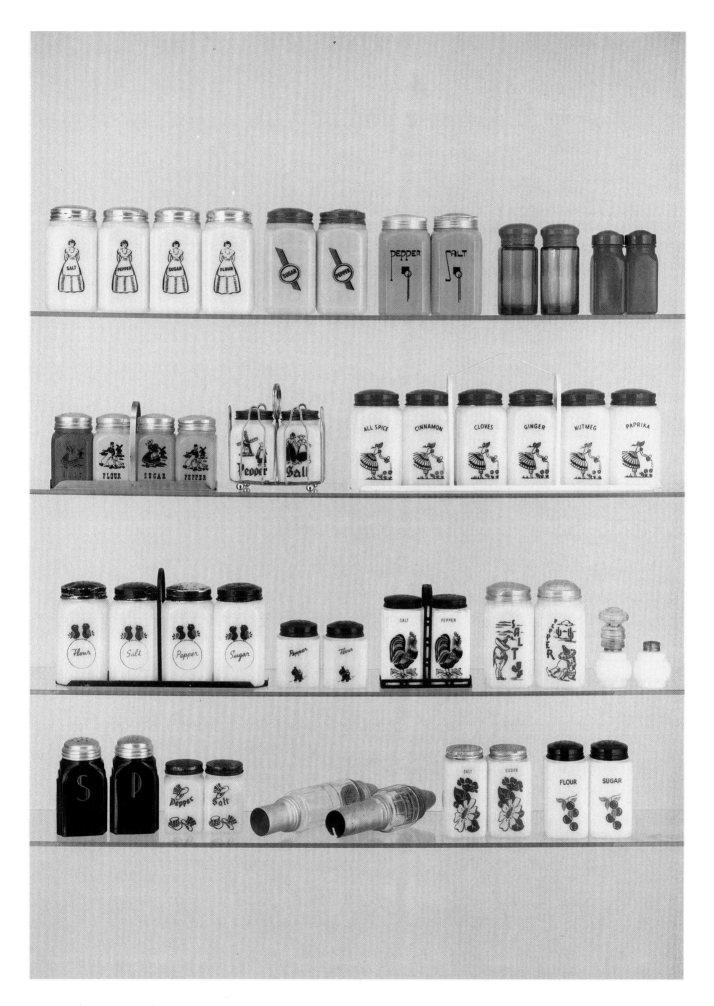

SHAKERS, JEANNETTE, McKEE, etc.

Availability of many of these type shakers has decreased in recent years. There are more salt and peppers found than other shakers, but one major problem with these heavily used items is worn lettering. Mint lettering on salt shakers is a premium! There were fewer flour, sugar and spice sets made than salt and pepper sets. Possibly extra shakers came with grease sets and possibly, ladies just did not buy shakers for flour and sugar!

All blue shakers are in demand, but there has also been an increase in demand for white and the later issued Fire King sets. New collectors start with the inexpensive sets and graduate to higher priced sets. Generally speaking, it would be better to buy the more expensive sets first!

Jeannette Glass Company (first 4½ rows)
Page 175

Row 1:	#1, 2	Delphite blue, 8 oz., salt or pepper, ea.	18.00–20.00
	#3	Same, sugar	35.00–40.00
	#4	Same, paprika	40.00–45.00
	#5, 6	Jadite, decorated salt/pepper, ea.	13.00–15.00
	#7, 8	Same, mouth wash or bicarbonate soda	30.00–35.00
	#9, 10	Jadite, 6 oz. w/o label, ea.	4.00– 5.00
Row 2:	#1, 2	Jadite light, salt or pepper	8.00–10.00
	#3, 4	Same, flour or sugar	10.00–12.00
	#5	Jadite dark, pepper	9.00–11.00
	#6	Same, flour	11.00–13.00
	#7, 8	Delphite blue, square, salt or pepper	40.00–45.00
	#9	Same, flour or sugar	55.00–60.00
Row 3:	#1, 2	Jadite dark, square, salt or pepper	11.00–13.00
	#3, 4	Same, flour or sugar	13.00–16.00
	#5, 6	Jadite light, square, salt or pepper	8.00–10.00

Row 3:	(Continued)		
	#7, 8	Same, flour or sugar	12.00–15.00
	#9	"Jennyware" pink	18.00–20.00
Row 4:	#1-4	"Jennyware" ultra-marine (subtract $1.00 missing label), ea.	20.00–22.00
	#5-8	Same, crystal	6.00– 8.00
Row 5:	#1-4	"Jennyware" flat shaker, ea.	25.00–27.50
	#5	Same, crystal	18.00–20.00
	#6	Green, sold as sugar shaker	30.00–40.00
	#7	Unknown manufacturer, green "Zipper"	30.00–35.00
	#8	Green, plain	30.00–35.00
Row 6:	#1	Green, embossed flour	35.00–40.00
	#2	Crystal, embossed salt	15.00–18.00
	#3	Crystal, embossed allspice	15.00–18.00
	#4	Crystal, embossed cinnamon	15.00–18.00
	#5	Crystal, ribbed	8.00–10.00
	#6-11	Sneath green, ea.	30.00–35.00

McKee "Roman Arch" Shakers
Page 176

Row 1:	#1	Skokie green, salt	20.00–22.50
	#2-4	Same, pepper, flour or sugar	15.00–18.00
	#5	Same, cinnamon	30.00–35.00
	#6, 7	Delphite blue, salt or pepper	45.00–50.00
	#8-10	Fired-on colors, ea.	8.00– 10.00
Row 2:	#1-4	"Dots" green	11.00–14.00
	#5-9	Same, blue or red	15.00–17.00
	#10	Custard w/green flour	8.00–10.00
Row 3:	#1, 2	Custard salt or pepper	10.00–12.00
	#3, 4	Same, flour or sugar	12.00–15.00
	#5, 6	"Diamond Check," pr. on white	25.00–30.00

Row 3:	(Continued)		
	#7, 8	"Dots" on white, pr.	20.00–24.00
	#9, 10	Fired-on red, pr.	16.00–20.00
Row 4:	#1-4	White w/black, ea.	10.00–12.00
	#5-7	White w/red, ea.	9.00–11.00
	#8, 9	Crystal, frosted, ea.	6.00– 7.00
Row 5:	#1-11	Black, pepper ($10.00-12.00) all others w/good lettering	12.00–15.00
		Black w/o lettering	5.00– 6.00
Row 6:	#1-4	Fired-on colored set	16.00–20.00
	#5	"Bow," red on white	10.00–12.00
	#6-9	"Ships," ea.	8.00– 9.00

McKee "Square" Shakers
Page 177

Row 1:	#1-3	Large, 16 oz., ea.	35.00–40.00
	#4-7	Small, 8 oz., ea.	10.00–12.00
	#8, 9	Skokie green, pr.	20.00–25.00
Row 2:	#1, 2	Embossed dark jade salt or pepper	28.00–30.00
	#3, 4	Same, flour or sugar	30.00–35.00
	#5	Embossed Chalaine blue, flour $60.00-65.00; others	70.00–75.00
	#6-9	Chalaine blue, ea.	30.00–35.00
Row 3:	#1-3	White, ea.	7.00– 9.00
	#4-8	"HOTPOINT" or "ELECTROCHEF" embossed white, ea.	6.00– 8.00
	#9, 10	White, ea.	7.00– 9.00

Row 4:	#1-7	Skokie green light or dark, ea.	8.00–10.00
	#8	Same, "Cinnamon"	22.00–25.00
	#9, 10	Black w/o good lettering ($8.00-10.00) w/lettering, ea.	14.00–15.00
Row 5:	#1, 2	Custard, ea. salt or pepper	10.00–12.00
	#3, 4	Flour or sugar	14.00–16.00
	#5, 6	Same, ginger, cinnamon, nutmeg w/good lettering, ea.	20.00–22.00
	#8	Seville yellow, salt or pepper	10.00–12.00
	#9, 10	Same, flour or sugar	12.00–14.00
Row 6:	#1, 2	Seville yellow, salt or pepper	10.00–12.00
	#3, 4	Same, flour or sugar	12.00–14.00
	#5-8	Skokie green, dark, ea.	8.00–10.00

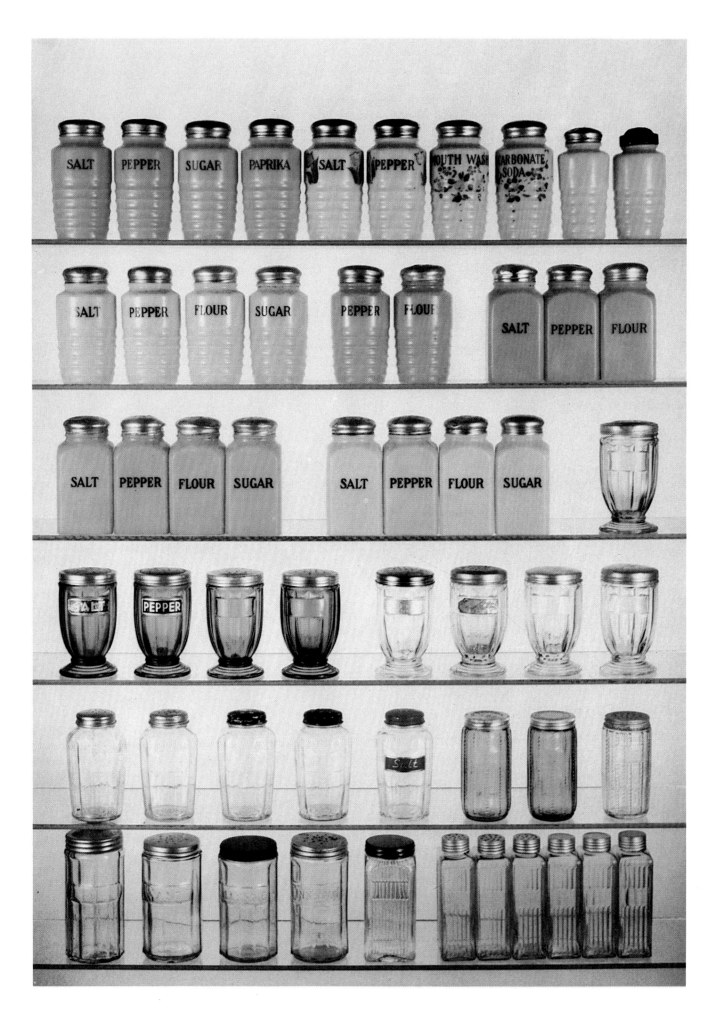

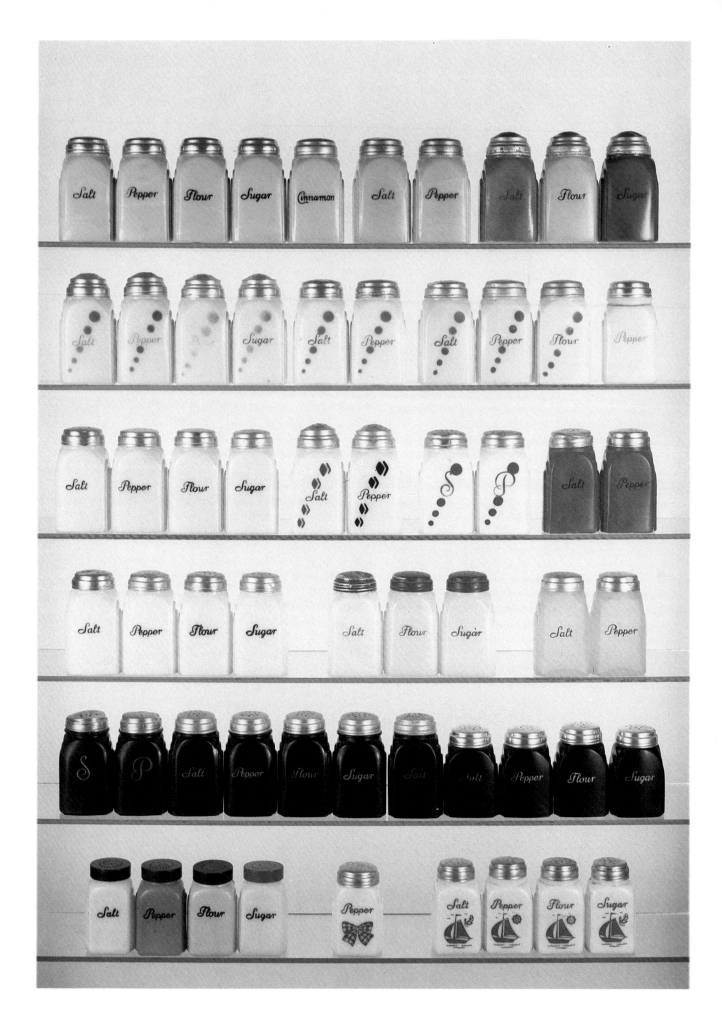

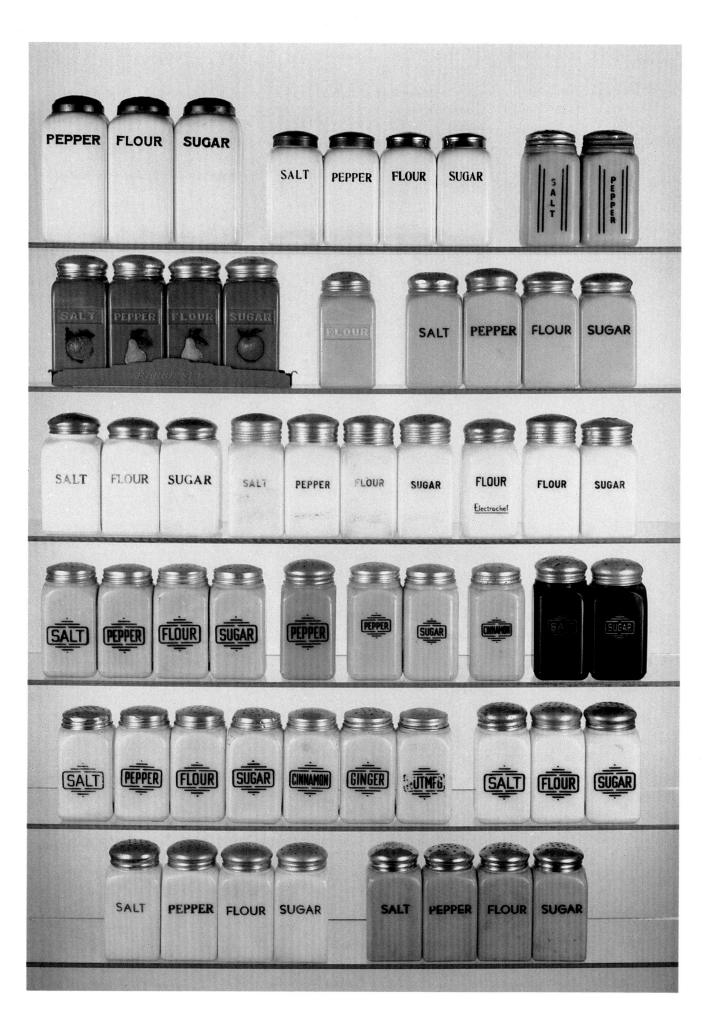

STRAW HOLDERS and Miscellaneous Late Arrivals

Straw jars are among the items that can be found at Antique advertising shows. Many collectors have one of these "soda fountain" remembrances, today. We have one in our kitchen that had a lot of use when the kids were younger. They couldn't drink a beverage without a straw.

The third straw holder in the top row on page 179 is quite a find. It is "Coca Cola" decorated! (Yes, it is an old one!)

Page 181 is an assortment of items gathered after three major photography sessions were completed. I could not wait for the next book to show you some of these such as the red, signed "Hawkes," sugar shaker.

Page 179

Row 1:	#1	Crystal, "Pattern Glass," zipper design, w/lid	225.00– 275.00
	#2	Crystal, w/metal base and lid (lid put on Greek Key jar on page 180 by mistake)	100.00– 125.00
	#3	Emerald Green "Coca Cola"	750.00–1,000.00
	#4	Crystal knobbed lid (Candlewick collectors notice this first)	150.00– 200.00
	#5	Crystal, "Pattern Glass," w/lid	200.00– 250.00
Row 2:	#1	Red, later made, possibly late 1950's/early 1960's	150.00– 200.00
	#2	Crystal, jointed straw lifter	100.00– 125.00
	#3	Crystal, named "Manhattan"	150.00– 200.00
	#4	Crystal, cut design on jar	175.00– 225.00
	#5	Crystal, zippered design, missing lid	75.00– 100.00
	#6	Amber, "English Hobnail," vase or straw jar	75.00– 90.00

Page 180

Row 1:	#1	Cobalt blue, 12" (vase or straw jar?)	250.00–275.00
	#2, 3	Crystal Heisey w/top	225.00–275.00
	#4	Crystal Heisey "Greek Key" w/o lid (metal lid belongs page 179, Row 1, #2) w/glass lid	125.00–150.00 / 275.00–300.00
	#5	Pink, Imperial vase (used as straw jar, but is vase)	65.00– 75.00
Row 2:	#1	Crystal, w/metal base	175.00–200.00
	#2	Crystal	75.00– 90.00
	#3	Green, short	300.00–325.00
	#4	Green, tall	325.00–350.00
	#5	Crystal, tall	100.00–135.00

Page 181

Row 1:	#1	"Pyrex" red bottle	25.00– 35.00
	#2	Cobalt, large jar, L.E. Smith	40.00– 45.00
	#3	Jadite decorated Coffee, Jeannette	30.00– 35.00
	#4	Red sugar shaker, signed "Hawkes"	300.00–350.00
	#5	Pink sugar shaker	35.00– 45.00
	#6	Ultra-marine electric beater	50.00– 60.00
Row 2:	#1	Mixing bowl, 7½", kitchen utensils decor	12.50– 15.00
	#2	"Red Willow" decorated, 5" bowl, Hazel Atlas	15.00– 17.50
	#3	Pink spoonholder, marked "Clamborne"	20.00– 25.00
	#4, 5	Cambridge sugar cube tray, pink or green	40.00– 50.00
Row 3:	#1	Chalaine blue mixing bowl, 9"	45.00– 55.00
	#2	Iridized, 9½", mixing bowl, Federal	15.00– 20.00
	#3	Amethyst, 9⅝" mixing bowl, Hazel Atlas	20.00– 22.50
Row 4:	#1	"White King" dispenser	100.00–125.00
	#2	"Sanitol" jar	10.00– 12.50
	#3	Colonial Block creamer	40.00– 50.00
	#4	Peacock blue measure cup	150.00–200.00
	#5	Cobalt blue creamer, "Chevron" like stripes	7.50– 8.50
	#6	Same, milk pitcher	9.00– 11.00

SUGAR SHAKERS

The bullet shaped sugar shakers with indented dots near the top have been found with McKee papers.

Page 183

Row 1: #1, 2   Cambridge, #732, pink (ewer
        cream $30.00-35.00)   100.00–115.00
     #3, 4   Cambridge #732, green (tall
        ewer cream $30.00-35.00)   110.00–125.00
     #5   Cambridge, blue   115.00–135.00
     #6, 7   Cambridge, amber (syrup
        w/cover $40.00-45.00)   65.00– 85.00

Row 2: #1, 2   Cambridge, pink (ewer cream
        $20.00-25.00)   65.00– 85.00
     #3   Cambridge, amber, crystal foot
        & glass top   75.00– 90.00
     #4, 5   Same, pink (ewer cream
        $22.00-25.00)   85.00–100.00
     #6, 7   Heisey "Yeoman," pink (cream
        $20.00-25.00); (add $10.00-15.00
        w/glass top)   65.00– 75.00
     #8   Cobalt blue   150.00–175.00
     #9   Green, w/green screw-in top 150.00–165.00

Row 3: #1, 2   Green or pink, footed
        ("Tilt-a-spoon")   175.00–225.00
     #3, 4   Green, 2 shades, possibly
        Paden City   130.00–145.00
     #5   Same, cobalt blue   300.00–350.00

Row 3: (Continued)
     #6   Same, amber   110.00–135.00
     #7   Paden City, pinched in,
        amber   125.00–150.00
     #8   Same, green   95.00–110.00

Row 4: #1   Green, Hocking   50.00– 65.00
     #2   Green, Hocking   45.00– 55.00
     #3   Unknown   40.00– 45.00
     #4   Green, "Hex Optic"   85.00–100.00
     #5   Amber   45.00– 55.00
     #6   Unknown, pink   55.00– 65.00
     #7   Pink, w/red top   85.00–100.00
     #8   Paden City "Party Line," pink 65.00– 75.00

Row 5: #1   Crystal, Paden City, 2 part
        dispenser   15.00– 18.00
     #2   Crystal, L.E. Smith   30.00– 35.00
     #3   Crystal, "West Sanitary Automatic
        Sugar"   20.00– 25.00
     #4, 5   Crystal, Hazel Atlas & un-
        known, ea.   10.00– 12.50
     #6   Crystal, faintly marked
        "Czechoslovakia"   20.00– 25.00

Page 184

Row 1: #1   Lancaster Glass Co., "Beehive",
        green   125.00–150.00
     #2-7   "Bullet" shape made by both
        Jeannette & Paden City
     #2, 3   Green   85.00–100.00
     #4   Yellow   175.00–200.00
     #5   Pink   85.00–100.00
     #6   Crystal   18.00– 25.00
     #7   Pink   100.00–115.00

Row 2: #1, 2   Blue, pink "Monroe Mfg. Co.,
        Elgin, Ill., Pat Pend." (liquid) 85.00–100.00
     #3, 4   Green or pink, footed   85.00–100.00
     #5   Green   100.00–125.00

Row 3: #1   Jeannette, light jade   45.00– 55.00

Row 3: (Continued)
     #2-4   Same, pink decorated, green
        or yellowish jade, ea.   45.00– 55.00
     #5-7   Jeannette, pink or green   40.00– 50.00
     #6   Same, frosted pink   35.00– 40.00
     #8   Green, cone top   55.00– 65.00

Row 4: #1   White Clambroth   35.00– 40.00
     #2, 3   Green or pink   18.00– 20.00
     #4, 5   Orange or forest green   45.00– 60.00
     #6   Red   100.00–125.00
     #7   Amber, horseshoe pattern   35.00– 40.00
     #8   Green, older style   20.00– 25.00
     #9   Crystal, marked sugar &
        cinnamon   12.00– 15.00

Page 185

Row 1: #1   Yellow fired-on w/red top   18.00– 20.00
     #2   Crystal, McKee, indented
        dots at top   20.00– 25.00
     #3   Ultra-marine, Jeannette   200.00–225.00
     #4   Same, green   90.00–100.00
     #5   Cobalt blue   175.00–200.00
     #6   Crystal, cone top   22.50– 25.00
     #7   Fired-on red   15.00– 18.00

Row 2: #1   Amber   110.00–135.00
     #2   Pink   100.00–125.00
     #3   Black   225.00–250.00
     #4   Green   95.00–110.00
     #5   SCA (sun colored amethyst)   65.00– 75.00
     #6, 7   Hex Optic green or pink   125.00–140.00

Row 3: #1, 2   Heisey, pink or green   100.00–125.00
     #3   Same, crystal   50.00– 55.00
     #4   Green   75.00– 85.00
     #5   Pink, measured teaspoon   110.00–125.00
     #6   Blue, marked "Made in
        Japan" (New!)   5.00– 10.00
     #7, 8   Pink or green   50.00– 65.00

Row 4: #1   Green   85.00– 95.00

Row 4: (Continued)
     #2   Pink, Paden City "Rena"
        Line 154   90.00–100.00
     #3   Same, crystal   30.00– 35.00
     #4   Same, green   90.00–100.00
     #5   Amber   50.00– 60.00
     #6   Blue   60.00– 75.00
     #7   Amber   115.00–135.00

Row 5: #1   Pink, Jeannette   40.00– 45.00
     #2   Same, dark Jadite   50.00– 60.00
     #3   Green   25.00– 30.00
     #4   Forest green, Owens Illinois   10.00– 12.50
     #5   Green, individual sugar   30.00– 35.00
     #6   Same, amber   45.00– 50.00
     #7   Green, handled   65.00– 75.00

Row 6: #1   Crystal, decorated flowers   12.50– 15.00
     #2   Crystal "Rena" Line, Paden
        City   12.50– 15.00
     #3   Crystal, zippered design   8.00– 10.00
     #4, 8   Crystal, ea.   15.00– 18.00
     #5   Crystal, Fostoria "American"   35.00– 40.00
     #7   Crystal, "Beehive"   25.00– 30.00

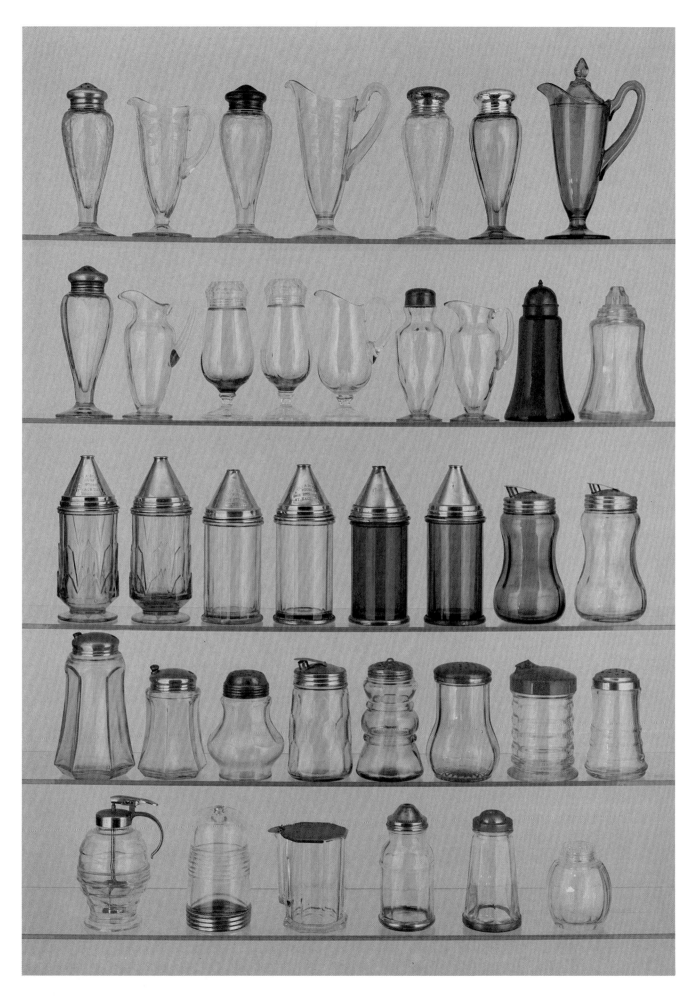

SYRUP PITCHERS

I've often remarked on the fact that many Depression Glass collectors are "item" collectors; however, the number of people I've encountered in my travels who collect syrup pitchers is amazing even to me. Somewhere in the course of conversation, they generally speak of attractive displays or fascinating shapes and colors. Generally, they carry pictures!

I recently bought a large Depression and Elegant glass collection. The collector sold me years of glass accumulation, but he kept his large syrup collection. In fact, I have never been able to buy a syrup pitcher collection. Once collected, these items seem to remain cherished.

Row 1:	#1	Cambridge, w/cover, amber	50.00– 55.00
	#2	Same, green	60.00– 65.00
	#3	Paden City, green	25.00– 30.00
	#4	Imperial, w/slotted lid, pink	55.00– 65.00
	#5	Same, amber	55.00– 65.00
Row 2:	#1	Hazel Atlas, pink	40.00– 45.00
	#2	Same, green	20.00– 25.00
	#3	Same, pink	40.00– 45.00
	#4	Hazel Atlas, pink	37.50– 42.50
	#5	Hazel Atlas, green	35.00– 40.00
	#6	Same, pink	37.50– 42.50
Row 3:	#1, 2	Fostoria "Mayfair," green or pink w/underliner	55.00– 65.00
	#3	Fostoria "Chintz"	150.00–160.00
	#4	Fostoria, "Mayfair," yellow w/underliner	55.00– 65.00
	#5	Same, amber	50.00– 60.00
Row 4:	#1	Pink	40.00– 45.00
	#2	Green w/liner	40.00– 50.00
	#3	Imperial, pink	45.00– 50.00
	#4	Imperial, pink w/floral cutting	40.00– 45.00
	#5	Same, green, plain	40.00– 45.00
Row 5:	#1	Paden City #198, 8 oz., amber	40.00– 50.00
	#2	Same, green	30.00– 35.00
	#3	Same, pink	30.00– 35.00
	#4	Paden City "Party Line," green	32.50– 37.50
	#5	Same, pink	32.50– 35.00
	#6	Paden City #198, 12 oz. green w/liner	40.00– 45.00

SYRUP PITCHERS Continued

Row 1:	#1	Crystal	10.00– 12.50
	#2	Green (possibly U.S. Glass)	30.00– 35.00
	#3	Standard Glass, pink	30.00– 35.00
	#4	Hocking, green swirl	35.00– 38.00
	#5, 6	Crystal, ea.	8.00– 10.00
Row 2:	#1	Amber/yellow combination w/glass lid	40.00– 45.00
	#2	Pink w/green knob, handle & pink underliner	40.00– 50.00
	#3	Duncan & Miller "Caribbean," blue	110.00–125.00
	#4	Same, crystal	55.00– 65.00
	#5	Cambridge, amber	30.00– 35.00
Row 3:	#1	Paden City, green floral cutting w/underliner	30.00– 35.00
	#2	Same, pink	32.50– 37.50
	#3	Same, pink w/painted flowers	35.00– 40.00
	#4	Cambridge, pink	30.00– 35.00
	#5	McKee, forest green	30.00– 35.00
Row 4:	#1, 3	Cambridge etched design w/underliner, pink	50.00– 60.00
	#2	Same, green	45.00– 55.00
	#4	Same, amber	45.00– 50.00
	#5	Cambridge, etched "Cleo"	115.00–135.00
Row 5:	#1	Cambridge, "Tally Ho" amber	40.00– 50.00
	#2	Cambridge, pink	45.00– 55.00
	#3	Same, amber	40.00– 50.00
	#4	Cambridge, amber	45.00– 50.00
	#5	Crystal, with crystal top	15.00– 18.00
	#6	Fenton, black	40.00– 50.00
Row 6:	#1	Heisey, "Moongleam" green	50.00– 65.00
	#2	Heisey, "Sahara" yellow	65.00– 75.00
	#3	Same, crystal	35.00– 40.00
	#4	Heisey, "Flamingo" pink	40.00– 45.00
	#5	Same, "Moongleam" green	45.00– 50.00
	#6	U.S. Glass miniature syrup, crystal	50.00– 60.00

WATER BOTTLES

There are many types of water containers shown throughout this book. Most water bottles have gone the way of ice boxes.

The "RADIUM EMANATOR FILTER" bottle shown below is an interesting find. In its original McKee carton, there is an empty space where the radium filter was to have been placed. The set is made up of a 12" bottle (marked "Radium Emanator Filter Co. Inc. North Haledonn, N.J.) which turns up onto another 12½" bottle. The total filtering system stands 21" tall. The "Canary Yellow" color is called vaseline by collectors. This bottle set sells for $300.00–350.00.

Row 1:	#1	"Water Falls"	15.00–18.00
	#2	"Water"	10.00–12.00
	#3	"G.E." shows old refrigerator	15.00–18.00
	#4	"Well," amber	45.00–55.00
	#5	"Ships"	12.00–15.00
Row 2:	#1	Owen-Illinois "Juice" on one side & "Water" on other	3.00– 5.00
	#2	Forest green "Penguin"	12.00–15.00
	#3	Lattice design w/lid	45.00–50.00
	#4	Hocking "Royal Ruby"	50.00–65.00
	#5	"G.E." round	6.00– 8.00
Row 3:	#1	"Crisscross," crystal	4.00– 5.00
	#2	"The Well Informed Choose Ice Refrigeration"	8.00–10.00
	#3	"Beveragette," Pat. 1919	12.00–15.00
	#4	Cobalt blue, 64 oz., 10" tall	55.00–60.00
	#5	Same, 32 oz.	35.00–40.00

Part 3 – Patterns & Companies

"CRISSCROSS," Hazel Atlas Glass Company, 1936-1938

"Crisscross" first attracted collectors because of the blue color. Now there are advocates for all the colors including crystal which is often mixed with one of the other colors for a more varied appearance.

Unlike in the last book, there has only been one newly discovered piece in "Crisscross." The 5½" round bowl has now been found in cobalt. You can see it with a crystal top on page 195. We could not find a cobalt top for the picture; but, rest assured, it does exist.

Pink tumblers are still elusive as are all the sugar and creamers in color. No one has found a sugar and creamer in blue – as yet. Nor have there been blue tumblers found to go with the pitchers. Those of you who collect other patterns of Depression era glass know how frustrating it is to collect a pattern which has a pitcher with no tumblers or vice versa.

Cobalt blue mixing bowls are just not being found as in the past. This has caused the prices to rise to the point that many collectors are settling for buying the smaller mixing bowls and forgetting the two larger sizes.

One thing that confuses new collectors is the difference in the pound butter and the refrigerator dish that is like the butter. Look at the picture on page 195. The butter in Row 4 has a bottom which sticks out with tabs. The top of the refrigerator dish is flush with the edges of the bottom as seen in Row 3.

	Blue	Crystal	Green	Pink
Bottle, water, 32 oz.	—	3.00–14.00	90.00–100.00	—
Bottle, water, 64 oz.	—	4.00– 5.00	100.00–125.00	—
Bowl, mixing set (5)	130.00-150.00	30.00–40.00	62.00– 75.00	62.00– 75.00
Bowl, mixing, 6⅝"	14.00– 16.00	3.00– 4.00	8.00– 10.00	8.00– 10.00
Bowl, mixing, 7⅝"	16.00– 18.00	4.00– 5.00	10.00– 12.00	10.00– 12.00
Bowl, mixing, 8¾"	20.00– 22.00	6.00– 7.00	14.00– 16.00	14.00– 16.00
Bowl, mixing, 9⅝"	18.00– 20.00	6.00– 7.00	10.00– 12.00	10.00– 12.00
Bowl, mixing, 10⅝"	60.00– 75.00	12.00–15.00	20.00– 25.00	20.00– 25.00
Butter, ¼ lb.	70.00– 80.00	10.00–12.00	30.00– 35.00	30.00– 35.00
Butter, 1 lb.	75.00– 85.00	15.00–18.00	30.00– 35.00	30.00– 35.00
Creamer	—	4.00– 5.00	25.00– 30.00	15.00– 20.00
Food mixer (baby face)	—	25.00–30.00	—	—
Pitcher, 54 oz.	500.00–600.00	70.00–85.00	—	—
Reamer, lemon	—	3.00– 5.00	9.00– 11.00	225.00–275.00
Reamer, orange	200.00–225.00	5.00– 8.00	10.00– 12.00	175.00–200.00
Refrigerator bowl, round 5½" w/cover	90.00–100.00	3.00– 4.00	75.00– 85.00	75.00– 85.00
Refrigerator bowl, w/cover				
4" x 4"	22.50– 25.00	2.00– 3.00	12.00– 15.00	8.00– 10.00
4" x 8"	55.00– 60.00	3.00– 4.00	20.00– 22.00	15.00– 18.00
8" x 8"	75.00– 85.00	4.00– 5.00	30.00– 35.00	40.00– 45.00
Refrigerator dish (like butter),				
3½" x 5¾"	60.00– 70.00	12.00–15.00	35.00– 40.00	—
Sugar	—	12.50–15.00	20.00– 25.00	20.00– 25.00
Sugar lid	—	17.50–20.00	30.00– 35.00	30.00– 35.00
Tumbler, 9 oz.	—	15.00–17.50	—	45.00– 50.00

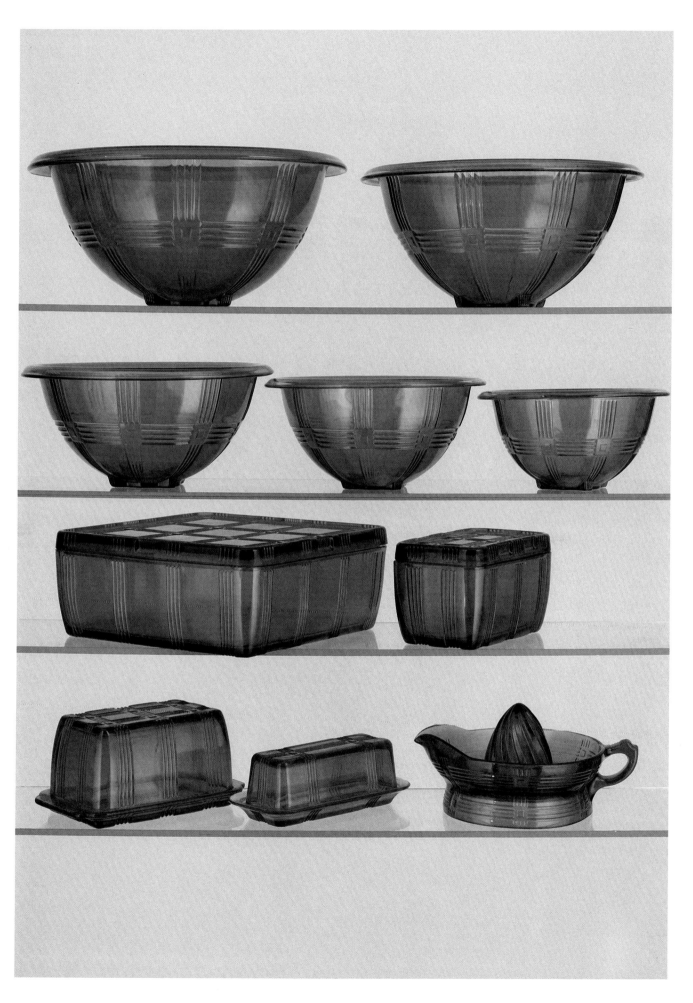

"DOTS," McKee Glass Company, 1930's–Early 1940's

McKee issued this as a "Deluxe" line of kitchenware and sold items to merchants from $4.00–12.00 per dozen. I have priced most items available although only a representative sampling can be seen on page 197.

Page 197

	Black/Green Dots on Custard	Blue/Red Dots on Custard	Dots on White
Bowl, 9", scalloped edge	22.00– 25.00	25.00– 30.00	17.50–20.00
Bowl, 9", w/spout	20.00– 22.50	25.50– 27.50	15.00–17.50
Bowl, drippings	25.00– 30.00	30.00– 35.00	18.00–20.00
Bowl, egg beater w/lip	15.00– 18.00	20.00– 22.50	11.00–13.00
Butter dish, 1 pound	85.00–100.00	85.00–100.00	35.00–40.00
Canister, 48 oz., screw lid	50.00– 57.50	55.00– 65.00	35.00–40.00
Canister, 28 oz., screw lid	37.50– 45.00	40.00– 45.00	20.00–25.00
Canister & lid, round, 48 oz.	20.00– 22.50	22.50– 25.00	15.00–18.00
Canister & lid, round, 40 oz.	18.00– 20.00	20.00– 22.50	12.00–15.00
Canister & lid, round, 24 oz.	16.00– 18.00	18.00– 20.00	10.00–12.00
Canister & lid, round, 10 oz.	13.00– 15.00	16.00– 18.00	10.00–12.00
Mixing bowl, 9"	14.00– 16.00	17.50– 20.00	10.00–12.50
Mixing bowl, 8"	12.00– 14.00	15.00– 17.50	9.00–11.00
Mixing bowl, 7"	10.00– 12.00	12.00– 15.00	7.50– 9.00
Mixing bowl, 6"	8.00– 10.00	10.00– 12.50	6.50– 7.50
Pitcher, 2 cup	30.00– 35.00	30.00– 35.00	22.00–25.00
Refrigerator dish, 4" x 5"	12.50– 15.00	12.50– 15.00	6.50– 7.50
Refrigerator dish, 5" x 8"	15.00– 20.00	18.00– 20.00	10.00–12.50
Shaker, ea.	11.00– 14.00	15.00– 17.00	10.00–12.00

"DOTS," Hazel Atlas & Hocking Glass Companies '30's - '50's

Dot designed kitchenware was made by several companies. The later made Fire King "Dots" in red and black are becoming very popular. I even received a photo of two red dotted 7½" mixing bowls incorporated into a chafing dish arrangement. The bowls were in a metal holder with candles under each and had metal lids covering them.

Page 198

Row 1:	#1	Hazel Atlas bowl, 9", red	15.00–18.00	*Row 3:*	#1	Hocking red bowl, 9½"	10.00–12.00
	#2	Same, 8"	12.00–15.00			Same, 8½" (not shown)	8.00–10.00
	#3	Hazel Atlas pitcher, 2 cup	30.00–35.00		#2	Same, 7½"	5.00– 7.00
	#4	Pitcher, ribbed 2 cup	20.00–22.50		#3	Same, 6½"	3.00– 4.00
Row 2:	#1	Hazel Atlas bowl, 8", yellow	12.00–15.00	*Row 4:*	#1	Hocking "Apple," 9½"	9.00–11.00
	#2	Same, 6"	8.00– 9.50			Same, 8½" (not shown)	8.00–10.00
		Same, 7" (not shown)	10.00–12.00			Same, 7½" (not shown)	5.00– 7.00
	#3	Same, 5"	5.00– 6.50		#2	Same, 6½"	3.00– 4.00
	#4	Hocking grease jar	12.50–15.00				

FIRE-KING Anchor Hocking Glass Company, Late 40'S - 60's

Anchor Hocking's "Tulips" design was one of their more popular patterns when issued. Because of its availability today, it still remains a popular pattern. Demand by collectors keeps the price up on patterns that are easily found.

Page 199

Row 1:	#1	"Tulips" bowl, 9½"	12.00–15.00	*Row 3:*	#1	"Fruits" bowl, 8½"	8.00–10.00
	#2	Same, 8½"	10.00–12.00			Same, 9½" (not shown)	10.00–12.00
	#3	Same, 7½"	6.00– 7.50		#2	Same, 7½"	5.00– 7.00
Row 2:	#1	Same, 6½"	4.50– 6.00		#3	Same, 6½"	3.00– 4.00
	#2	Same, grease jar	10.00–12.50	*Row 4:*	#1	Red flashed, flower decorated casserole, 10 oz.	20.00–25.00
	#3	Same, shaker	4.00– 5.00		#2	Blue, 2 qt. cass., cut florals	25.00–30.00
	#4	Batter bowl, "Fruits" (peaches, grapes and pears)	15.00–17.50		#3	Jad-ite, 2 spout skillet	20.00–25.00

FIRE-KING

Row 1: #1 "Swedish Modern," "Turquoise Blue," 11" mixing bowl,
3 qt. 10.00–12.50

#2 Same, 9½", 2 qt. 9.00–10.00

#3 Same, 8", 1 qt. 7.00– 8.50

#4 Same, 6½", 1 pt., (not shown) 5.00– 6.50

Row 2: #1 "Splash Proof," "Turquoise Blue," 9½" mixing
bowl, 4 qt. 10.00–12.50

#2 Same, 8½", 3 qt. 8.00– 9.50

#3 Same, 7½", 2 qt. 6.50– 7.50

#4 Same, 6½", 1 qt., (not shown) 4.50– 5.50

Row 3: #1 "Splash Proof," "Fruit," 9½" mixing bowl, 4 qt. ... 10.00–12.00

#2 Same, 8½", 3 qt. 8.00–10.00

#3 Same, 7½", 2 qt. 5.00– 7.00

#4 Same, 6½", 1 qt., (not shown) 3.00– 4.00

Row 4: #1 "Ivory," 9⅛" deep loaf pan 5.00– 7.50

#2 Same, 6 oz. individual baker 1.00– 1.50

#3 Same, 9" cake pan 8.00–10.00

#4 Same, 10½" baking pan 7.00– 9.00

Row 5: #1 Jad-ite juice saver pie plate, 10⅜" 35.00–40.00

#2 Mug w/design on outside (no design $2.00-3.00) ... 20.00–22.50

#3 Jade-ite mixing bowl, 8" 4.00– 5.00

Same, 9" (not shown) 5.00– 7.00

#4 Same, 7" 3.00– 4.00

Same, 6" (not shown) 2.00– 3.00

FIRE-KING Sapphire Blue

Baker, 1 pt., round or square	3.50– 4.00	Cup, 8 oz measuring, 3 spout	15.00–18.00
Baker, 1 qt.	4.50– 5.00	Custard cup, 5 oz.	2.00– 3.00
Baker, 1½ qt.	8.50– 9.00	Custard cup, 6 oz., 2 styles	2.50– 3.50
Baker, 1 qt.	9.00– 10.00	Loaf pan, 9⅛", deep	18.00–20.00
Bowl, 5⅜", cereal or deep dish		Nurser, 4 oz.	10.00–12.00
pie plate	9.00– 11.00	Nurser, 8 oz.	14.00–17.50
Bowl, 4⅜", individual pie plate	8.00– 10.00	Pie plate, 8⅜"	6.00– 7.00
Bowl, 16 oz. measuring, 2 spout	15.00– 18.00	Pie plate, 9"	7.00– 8.00
Cake pan (deep), 8¾"	12.00– 15.00	Pie plate, 9⅝"	8.00– 9.00
Casserole, 1 pt., knob handle cover	8.00– 10.00	Pie plate, 10⅜", w/juice saver rim	50.00–60.00
Same, 1 qt.	9.00– 10.00	Percolator top, 2⅛"	3.00– 3.50
Same, 1½ qt.	10.00– 12.00	Refrigerator jar & cover, 4½" x 5"	7.00– 9.00
Same, 2 qt.	12.00– 15.00	Same, 5⅛" x 9⅛"	22.50–25.00
Casserole, individual, 10 oz.	10.00– 12.00	Roaster, 8¾"	30.00–35.00
Casserole, 1 qt., pie plate cover	12.50– 15.00	Roaster, 10⅜"	45.00–55.00
Same, 1½ qt.	12.50– 15.00	Table server, tab handles (hot plate)	12.00–15.00
Same, 2 qt.	15.00– 18.00	Utility bowl, 6⅞"	8.00–10.00
Coffee mug, 7 oz., 2 styles	16.00– 18.00	Utility bowl, 8⅜"	10.00–12.00
Cup, 8 oz., dry measure, no spout	100.00–125.00	Utility bowl, 10⅛"	13.00–15.00
Cup, 8 oz. measuring, 1 spout	12.00– 15.00	Utility pan, 8⅛" x 12½"	15.00–20.00

FRY GLASSWARE, H.C. Fry Glass Company, 1920's-1930's

The opalescent white color most people are familiar with was called "Pearl" by the factory. Decorated pieces are more desirable than the regular issues. The colors are all rarer than the "Pearl" with both blue shades ("Azure" and "Royal") the most in demand. Fry glass without the opalescent effect is called "lime glass." According to avid Fry collectors, ovenware condition is not as important as obtaining an important addition to a collection.

All dates or numbers listed are marked on the piece.

Page 205

Row 1: #1 Reamer, fluted, jello mold, "Canary" 200.00– 225.00
#2 Meat loaf w/lid, rectangular, 9" 40.00– 50.00
#3 Reamer, straight side 300.00– 325.00
Row 2: #1 Grill plate, 8½", "Rose" 25.00– 30.00
#2 Same, "Azure" blue 30.00– 40.00
#3 Measure cup, 3 spout, "Pearl" 55.00– 65.00
#4 Bean pot w/lid, 1 pt. 30.00– 35.00
Row 3: #1 Grill plate, 10½", "Rose" 40.00– 45.00
#2 Measure cup, 1 spout 40.00– 50.00
#3 Grill plate, 10½", "Pearl" w/blue trim 50.00– 65.00
Row 4: #1 Same, w/orange enamel trim 50.00– 65.00
#2 Reamer, straight side, "Azure" blue 1,250.00–1,500.00

Row 4: (Continued)
#3 Same as #1, "Royal" blue 50.00– 65.00
Row 5: #1 Meat platter, 13", green, "Not Heat Resisting Glass" 55.00– 70.00
#2 Percolator top w/blue finial 20.00– 25.00
#3 Snack plate, 6" x 9", w/cup "Royal" blue 50.00– 60.00
Row 6: #1 Same as Row 5 #1, 17" 85.00–100.00
#2 Percolator top w/green finial 20.00– 25.00
#3 Casserole, oval, 7", w/green trim 35.00– 45.00

Page 206

Row 1: #1 Domed roaster (1946-14) 14" x 10" x 7½" 100.00–125.00
#2 Same as #1 but in metal holder. Paper label reads: "This is a 'ROYALLOY' Steel Frame. Dry thoroughly after using and it will serve you well and long." 110.00–135.00

Row 2: **Sunnybrook Cookie Jar**
(Introduced at $0.57; original price $0.75)
#1 "Royal" blue 200.00–250.00
#2 Green 175.00–225.00
#3 "Rose" 150.00–175.00
#4 Black 200.00–250.00

Page 207

Row 1: #1 Bean pot w/lid, 1 qt. in holder 45.00–55.00
#2 Cream soup, 5¼", ftd. 35.00–45.00
#3 Casserole w/lid, 8" round, in holder 20.00–30.00
Row 2: #1 Casserole, oval, 10" w/green finial 50.00–60.00
#2 Sundae glass "MACO-MFG-CO, VAPOR-RITE, MAY-WOOD-ILL 55.00–70.00
#3 Oval platter, 9" x 13" 25.00–35.00
Row 3: #1 Casserole, 6" round 15.00–20.00
#2 Baker, 6" round 15.00–20.00
#3 Cocotte, 5" (for indiv. meat, chicken, oyster pies) 8.00–10.00
#4 Same, 4" 8.00–10.00
#5 Custard cup, 4½ oz. 4.00– 5.00
Row 4: #1 Snack plate, 6" x 9" w/cup 20.00–25.00
#2 Mushroom baker/round shirred egg, 6" 55.00–75.00

Row 4: (Continued)
#3 Baker, oval, 6" 25.00–30.00
#4 Apple baker or custard, 4¾" 12.00–15.00
Row 5: #1 Butter pat (?) "Fry's Heat Resisting Glass" 50.00–75.00
#2 Ramekin, 3" 6.00– 8.00
#3, 4 & 7 Custard cup, 4 or 6 oz. (1927 or 1936) 6.00– 8.00
#5, 6 Custard cup, 6 oz., engraved (1927 or 1936) 10.00–12.00
Row 6: #1 Casserole, 7" round, engraved w/blue finial 55.00–70.00
#2, 3 Ramekin "Pearl" or "Lime glass," ea. 6.00– 8.00
#4 Oval server, 8 sided, engraved, 6½" x 9"/holder 60.00–75.00

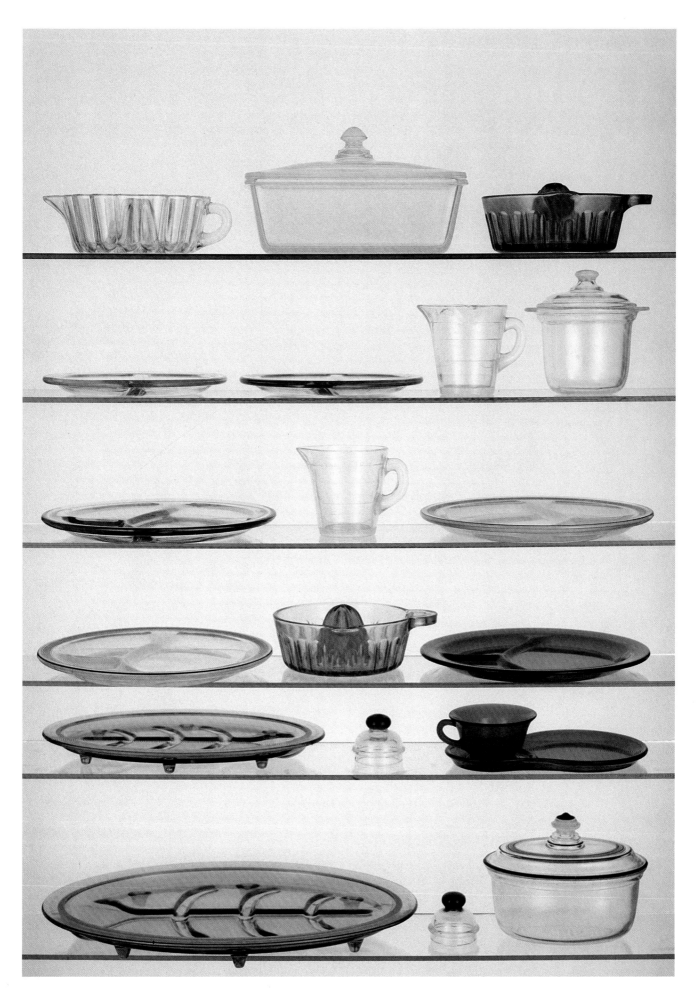

FRY GLASSWARE, H.C. Fry Glass Company 1920's-1930's

The antique business is a way to meet many interesting collectors from all over the country. At the Heisey Convention in 1988, I met a couple of avid Fry collectors on preview night. I had a stack of "Azure" blue small grills, cups and saucers that I had recently purchased. They were surprised to find that there were several dealers, besides me, who also had Fry for sale. We talked and they invited me to use any of their collection for a future book.

I would like to thank Hank and Carla Bowman for their help and use of their Fry glassware for this section as well as for providing valuable information for use in the book.

Most people in all collecting fields are more than willing to share glass and information. That is one of the more rewarding aspects of writing. I hope you gain knowledge to help your collecting from the long hours spent compiling this.

Row 5 consists of a child's set that was sold for $2.50 in 1922. It was called "Little Mother's Kidibake Set" and now sells for $275.00.

Page 209

Row 1:	#1	Casserole w/lid, 7" square, in holder	45.00–55.00
	#2	Baker, pudding, 2⅛" x 6⅜"	12.00–15.00
	#3	Casserole w/lid, 8" oval, engraved in holder	35.00–40.00
Row 2:	#1	Brown betty, 9"	40.00–45.00
	#2	Casserole w/lid, 7" round, engraved side & lid	50.00–55.00
		Trivet, 8" under casserole	15.00–17.50
	#3	Shirred egg, 7½", round	20.00–25.00
Row 3:	#1	Vegetable dish, 2 part, 9¾"	25.00–30.00
	#2	Fish platter, 11", engraved	30.00–35.00
	#3	Pie plate, 9½", engraved, in holder	35.00–45.00
Row 4:	#1	Cake, 9" round	15.00–20.00
	#2	Cup and saucer, No. 1969	35.00–40.00
	#3	Pie plate, 10" in metal holder	20.00–25.00
Row 5:	#1	Pie plate, 5"	40.00–50.00
	#2	Casserole w/lid, 4½" round	60.00–75.00
	#3,4	Ramekin, 2½", ea	30.00–40.00
	#5	Bread baker, 5"	55.00–70.00
Row 6:	#1	Fish platter, 17", engraved	30.00–40.00
	#2	Casserole w/lid, 7" round, embossed w/grapes	65.00–85.00

"JENNYWARE," Jeannette Glass Company, 1936-1938

"Jennyware" is popular with collectors due, in part, to the many different items that can be acquired. A major problem in collecting "Jennyware" is the variations of color occurring in ultra-marine. The greenish shade of "Jennyware" has few collectors. Dealers usually avoid buying that shade for resale.

That decanter in the top row was made by Imperial and is not a part of the "Jennyware" set. Many collectors buy it as a "go-with" item. It sells for $40.00-50.00.

Page 211, 212

	Crystal	Pink	Ultra-marine
Bowl, mixing set (3)	24.00–30.00	70.00– 80.00	90.00–105.00
Bowl, 10½"	10.00–12.50	30.00– 35.00	35.00– 45.00
Bowl, 8¼"	8.00–10.00	20.00– 22.50	35.00– 37.50
Bowl, 6"	6.00– 7.50	20.00– 22.50	20.00– 22.50
Butter dish, deep bottom	25.00–30.00	65.00– 70.00	85.00– 90.00
Butter dish, flat bottom	—	—	175.00–200.00
Coaster	—	5.00– 6.00	5.00– 6.00
Measuring cup set (4)	80.00–90.00	100.00–120.00	110.00–125.00
1 cup	25.00–30.00	32.00– 35.00	35.00– 40.00
½ cup	22.00–25.00	30.00– 35.00	32.00– 35.00
⅓ cup	17.50–20.00	22.50– 27.50	25.00– 30.00
¼ cup	12.00–15.00	15.00– 20.00	15.00– 20.00
Pitcher, 36 oz.	25.00–30.00	65.00– 70.00	75.00– 90.00
Reamer	60.00–75.00	60.00– 70.00	70.00– 80.00
Refrigerator dish, 70 oz., round	8.00–10.00	30.00– 35.00	30.00– 35.00
Refrigerator dish, 32 oz., round	6.00– 8.00	15.00– 18.00	16.00– 18.00
Refrigerator dish, 16 oz., round	4.00– 6.00	18.00– 20.00	18.00– 20.00
Refrigerator dish, 4½" x 4½"	4.00– 6.00	18.00– 20.00	20.00– 22.00
Refrigerator dish, 4½" x 9"	6.00– 8.00	25.00– 28.00	27.00– 30.00
Shaker, footed, ea.	6.00– 8.00	18.00– 20.00	20.00– 22.00
Shaker, flat, ea.	18.00–20.00	25.00– 28.00	—
Tumbler, 8 oz.	20.00–22.00	30.00– 35.00	35.00– 40.00

Pyrex Corning Glass Works

The boxed glassware shown here was discovered in early 1986 near Chicago. It is great to find new information! So keep looking and write me about your finds!

Page 213

Row 1:	#1	Pyrex 8 piece "Matched Set" #145 consisting of six 5 oz. custard cups, one 1½ qt. casserole w/pie plate cover in box	22.00–25.00
	#2	Pyrex 9 piece "Economy Set" #179 consisting of 8 oz. measuring cup, 9½" pie plate, six 4 oz. custards & handy cup rack	25.00–30.00
Row 2 & items 1 & 2 in Row 3:		Pyrex "Gift Set" #245 consisting of 8½" pie plate, 9⅛" loaf pan, 8⅝" cake dish, 10½" utility dish, six 4 oz. custards & 1½ qt. casserole in box	35.00–40.00
Row 3:	#3	Blue, 4¼" x 6¾" w/lid	25.00–30.00
	#4	Blue, milk pitcher	35.00–40.00
Row 4:	#1	Mixing bowl set, 6½", 7½", 8½"	15.00–18.00
	#2	Divided relish	12.50–15.00
	#3	Teapot, with floral cutting (marked "Corning Pyrex") in lid	50.00–60.00

"SHIPS," McKee Glass Company, 1930's

I might point out that the pitcher shown in the top row is not a part of the set, but it is a great "go-with" accessory. It sells for $25.00-30.00. Collectors still prefer white lids for their canisters; but if you use these, the clear tops are more convenient for viewing the contents of the dish! Black or red "Ships" are priced similarly.

Page 215

Bowl, drippings, 8 oz.	25.00–30.00	Mixing bowl set (4)	35.00–45.00
Bowl, drippings, 16 oz.	25.00–30.00	Mixing bowl, 9"	12.00–15.00
Bowl, drippings, rectangular (4" x 5")	25.00–30.00	Mixing bowl, 8"	10.00–12.00
Bowl, egg beater w/spout, 4½"	20.00–25.00	Mixing bowl, 7"	8.00–10.00
Bowl, beater w/spout, 6½"	22.50–25.00	Mixing bowl, 6"	6.00– 8.00
Butter dish	20.00–22.00	Pitcher, 2 cup	12.00–15.00
Canister & lid, round, 48 oz., 5"h	20.00–25.00	Refrigerator dish, 4" x 5"	10.00–12.00
Canister & lid, round, 46 oz., 4½"h	16.00–18.00	Refrigerator dish, 5" x 8"	14.00–16.00
Canister & lid, round, 24 oz., 3½"h	14.00–16.00	Shaker, ea.	8.00– 9.00
Canister & lid, round, 10 oz., 2½"h	12.00–14.00	Tumbler (or Egg Cup)	12.00–15.00

"SHIPS" and "DUTCH"

These categories are more related than you think. They share the same cabinets and home. Cathy collects both of these, and they are fun to find. You never know what unusual piece will surface. I carried that large Jadite windmill bowl on Page 216 for half a mile a couple of weeks before photography. I already had my arms full of purchases before I spotted it, and I regretted having seen it more than once, before I reached my car.

Page 216

Row 1:	#1	Jadite, 9¾" bowl, w/windmills	35.00–40.00	Row 2:	(Continued)	
	#2, 3	Hocking canister w/Dutch decal, ea.	15.00–20.00		#5-7 Tipp City Dutch shakers, ea.	4.00– 5.00
	#4	Hocking provision jar w/Dutch decal	12.50–15.00	Row 3:	#1 Black "Ships" beater bowl, 6½"	22.50–25.00
Row 2:	#1	Windmill "Drippings" (turned wrong)	20.00–25.00		#2 Same, 10 oz. canister	12.00–14.00
	#2	Dutch boy shaker	10.00–12.50		#3 Same, 24 oz.	14.00–16.00
	#3	Dutch boy and girl shakers w/holder	12.50–15.00		#4 Same, 46 oz.	16.00–18.00
	#4	"Churn lady" pr. shakers	10.00–12.50	Row 4:	#1 Same, refrigerator dish, 5" x 8"	15.00–18.00
					#2 Same, 4" x 5"	10.00–12.50
					#3 Same, 6" mixing bowl	6.00– 8.00

"DUTCH", "DUTCH", and more "DUTCH"

Page 217

Rows 1 & 2: **Hazel Atlas "Skating Dutch"**

	#1	One piece stack set	15.00–20.00	Row 3:	#1 Dutch/tulips/windmills, 9" mixing bowl	10.00–12.50
	#2	Three piece stack set	25.00–30.00		#2 Same, 8"	8.00–10.00
	#3	Mixing bowl, 9"	10.00–12.50		#3 Same, 7"	6.00– 7.50
	#4	Same, 8"	8.00–10.00		#4 Same, 6"	5.00– 6.00
Row 2:	#1	Same, 7"	6.00– 7.50	Row 4:	#1 Same, 5"	4.00– 5.00
	#2	Same, 6"	5.00– 6.00		#2 Fired-on Dutch set w/holder, 3"	25.00–30.00
	#3	Same, 5"	4.00– 5.00		#3 Same set, 4"	35.00–40.00
	#4	Cereal bowl, 5"	4.00– 5.00			
	#5	Salt and pepper pr.	14.00–16.00			

LATE ARRIVALS and REPRODUCTIONS

No matter how much planning and foresight goes into a photography session, there are always a few pieces that get omitted, inadvertently forgotten or do not seem to fit the page being photographed at the time. Page 219 is representative of such from our four day West Coast photo session.

Page 219

Row 1: #1 Pink "SELLERS" canister 100.00–125.00
     #2 Recent 6¼" canister,
         cobalt blue 20.00– 25.00
     #3 Restwell 9¾", mixing bowl,
         cobalt blue 60.00– 75.00
Row 2: #1 Paden City "Party Line,"
         blue ice tub 40.00– 50.00
     #2 Ultra-marine sugar 125.00–150.00
     #3 Peacock blue 3¾" jar 15.00– 20.00
     #4 Same, 4¾" 25.00– 30.00
     #5 Blue jelly jar 12.00– 15.00
     #6 Green 4½" tumbler
         (mission juice) 12.00– 15.00
Row 3: #1 Soap dish "Ivory Soap,"
         blue 45.00– 50.00
     #2 Custard fruit jar 25.00– 35.00
     #3 Pyrex, mug "Canada" 20.00– 25.00
     #4 Hocking, blue vase 10.00– 12.00
     #5-7 Spice jars, "Best Because
         Pure," embossed Allspice,
         Ginger, Soda; light blue,
         ea. 12.50– 15.00

Row 4: #1 Glasbake, 5½" tall, 6" diam.
         jar w/lid 20.00– 25.00
     #2 Glasbake, 4¾" tall 5" diam.
         jar w/lid 15.00– 20.00
     #3 Glasbake, two handled
         baker 6.00– 8.00
     #4 Embossed "Ginger" spice
         canister 15.00– 20.00
     #5 Paden City, etched blue
         decanter 40.00– 45.00
Row 5: #1 Glasbake casserole w/lid 18.00– 20.00
     #2 Holt soap dish, blue 20.00– 25.00
     #3 Cobalt blue percolator
         top 15.00– 20.00
     #4 Canister, 4¾" part of set
         w/#2 top row 12.50– 15.00
     #5 Same, 3¾" 12.50– 15.00
     #6 Same, 3¼" 10.00– 12.50

Page 220

Row 1: #1 BROMO-SELTZER "two
         way" advertising sign
         display 125.00–150.00
     #2 Seville yellow "Cookie
         Jar" 200.00–300.00

Row 2: #1, 3 Shakers, patriotic "God
         Bless America;" "It's Great
         to be an American" 12.00–15.00
     #2 Butter dish, Lincoln picture 30.00–35.00

REPRODUCTIONS – BARNES REAMERS

This picture shows the colors of Barnes (made for Edna Barnes of Uniontown, Ohio) reamers issued as of December 1988. THESE ARE LIMITED EDITION REAMERS. They are collectible in their own right. Some colors are sold out and are selling above the issue price.

Page 221

Rows 1-3: See Page 134-135 for original colors. Both the top (inside cone) and the bottom (on the base) are marked with a **B** in a circle. A few of the cobalt blue are marked with an N and not a B, so be aware of that. These will be listed in order they were made. (Some are satinized or frosted).

#1 Cobalt   Row 1, #1
#2 Rubina   Row 2, #3
#3 Vaseline & frosted   Row 1, #2, 3
#4 Black   Row 3, #1
#5 Apple green & frosted   Row 2, #1, 2
#6 Cranberry Ice & frosted Row 1, #4, 5

#7 Gold & frosted   Row 2, #4, 5
#8 Blue Bell & frosted   Row 3, #2, 3
#9 White Milk & painted blue & Row 3, #4, 5
     painted pink flowers also
#10 Aqua & frosted (made early 1989)
#11 Red to be made in 1989.

Rows 4-8: Show Barnes reamers which are called 5" and 2½", but really measure 4¾" and 2¼". There is a **B** in a circle on the tab handle of both sizes. Some of these have also been frosted.

Row 1: Heatherbloom, Custard, Green Carnival,
     Forest Green
Row 2: Cobalt, Sapphire, Harvest Swirl

Row 3: Cranberry Ice, Gold, Pink Rosemarie
Row 4: Red Glow, Depression Green, Chocolate

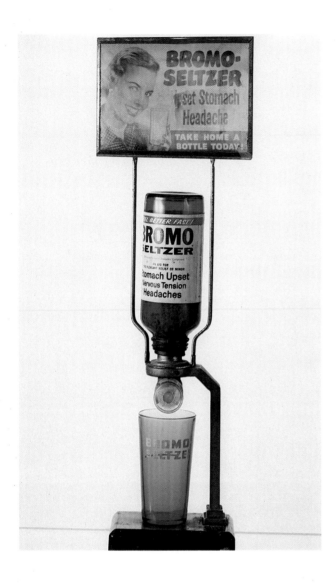

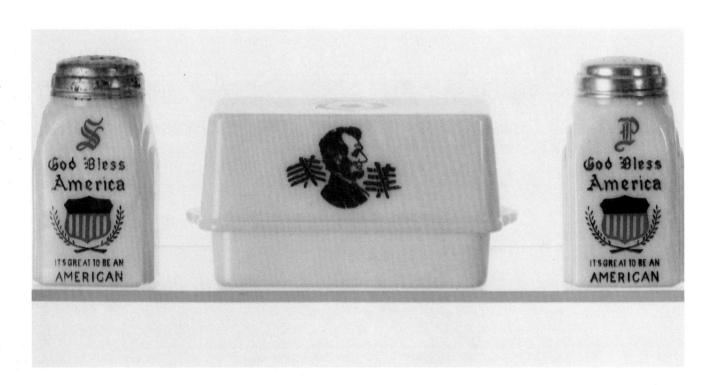

REPRODUCTIONS and NEWLY MADE ITEMS

Three years ago, when I wrote the third edition of *Kitchen Glassware,* there were only a few Kitchenware items to report as reproductions. With the demise of Westmoreland Glass Company and the sale of their glass moulds, a whole new world of reproductions appeared. I will approach each item shown on page 223 separately. These are all new! If you wish to purchase any of these, you need to realize that the price for newly made items is determined by seller demand and what the buyer is willing to pay. There is little structured market price especially on the "foreign" made "rip-offs."

The colors shown or listed are current at this writing (Spring 1989); but do not be surprised at any color appearing in these items. Know your dealer if you do not know the merchandise! Subscribe to a national trade paper to keep abreast of the latest happenings. (See page 224.)

Row 1: #1-3 – Westmoreland w/oranges and lemons being made by Summit Art Glass in colors of black, "Moonlight" blue, cobalt blue and recently in "vaseline." Original moulds are being used and only pink, green and crystal were made originally.

Row 1: #4, 5 – Hazel Atlas 2 cup reamer being made in Far East (likely Taiwan) in green, cobalt blue and pink. THIS IS A MAJOR PROBLEM! Even reamer collectors are having difficulty with this one. The green is easily seen by the horrible color; the pink and blue are fairly true to the originals. They are good copies! The repros all have an oily slick feel and are slightly heavier than the older ones. The repros are wavy and lettering on the sides is slightly different. However, it is impossible to tell you a sure way to tell the old from the new in words that you can feel safe in buying these. I can only emphasize to know who you are dealing with and if the price seems reasonable on an expensive piece, then there might be a good reason. **BUYER BEWARE!**

Row 2: #1-4 – Easley pat July 10 1888, Sept 10, 1888. Never made in color originally. Original crystal sells $12.00–15.00.

Row 2: #5 – Hazel Atlas cobalt blue three spout, one cup measuring cup made in Taiwan. Spouts are not smoothly made, but is a good copy.

Row 2: #6 – Hazel Atlas "Kellogg's" embossed cup was made in green and pink in Taiwan. Major difference is on 4 in 4 oz. measurement on side. In old, line forming 4 crosses in middle of 4 while on new the perpendicular line crosses ¾ of the way down the 4 in the 4 oz.

Row 3: #1-5 – Gillispie cup w/reamer top made by Summit Art Glass. Cup was never made in color and originally had a measure top instead of reamer top. (See page 109.)

Row 3: #6, 7 – Dry measure w/reamer top made by Summit Art Glass but heretofore, unknown.

Row 4: #1, 2 – Hazel Atlas shakers (salt and pepper) made in Taiwan. Never made in cobalt blue originally. Pink quality varies greatly as do designs. Stippling effect behind embossed salt or pepper is very pronounced on new. New tops are punched in circular pattern.

Row 4: #3 – Fostoria "Colony-like" two spout reamer made originally in white and crystal.

Row 4: #4-7 – Duboe Pat July 24, 1917 made by Summit and copied without markings in Taiwan. Never made in color originally and sells $40.00–50.00 in crystal.

Row 5: #1-4 – Made by Summit Art Glass from Westmoreland mould. Original colors are shown on page 149 in Rows 3-5. All additional colors are NEW!

Row 6: #1, 3 – Same as dry measures in Row 3: #6, 7 but spout pulled to make measure cup.

Row 6: #2 – Possible Westmoreland cup, footed and spouted and made by Summit in black.

Row 6: #4 – Same as Row 2 without reamer top.

Row 6: #5, 6 – Cobalt blue and black made for Barnes by Imperial in 1981. (Marked IG 81)

A publication I recommend:

Books By Gene Florence

Collector's Encyclopedia of Depression Glass $19.95

Pocket Guide to Depression Glass $9.95

Collector's Encyclopedia of Occupied Japan I $14.95

Collector's Encyclopedia of Occupied Japan II $14.95

Collector's Encyclopedia of Occupied Japan III $19.95

Elegant Glassware of the Depression Era $19.95

Very Rare Glassware of the Depression Years $24.95

The Standard Baseball Card Price Guide, 2nd Edition $9.95

Add $2.00 postage for the first book,
45¢ for each additional book.

Copies of these books may be ordered from:

Gene Florence
P.O. Box 22186
Lexington, KY 40522

or

Collector Books
P.O. Box 3009
Paducah, KY 42002-3009